What Readers are s

Kendra Smiley has written a b..... .. your life. In *Heart Clutter*, she offers practical advice, poignant illustrations, and biblical wisdom that will help you sort through your personal possessions and your deeply kept secrets and figure out what to let go of and what to keep.

♥**Carol Kent, Speaker and Author**
Unquenchable: Grow a Wildfire Faith that Endures

Kendra Smiley's wisdom, wit, and warmth make every word she writes a ray of sunshine into a woman's heart and soul. Your life will always be better and brighter with Kendra's insights in it.

♥**Pam Farrel, author of 40 books including** *Men are like Waffles Women are like Spaghetti* **and** *7 Simple Skills for Every Woman*

We all need to clear out our heart clutter on a regular basis—a task that can feel overwhelming at times—but Kendra Smiley shows us just how to do it! How to determine what to throw away, what to give away, and what to keep. On every page, she motivates us, encourages us, and cheers us on, every step of the way!

♥**Christin Ditchfield, Author of** *What Women Should Know About Letting It Go: Breaking Free From the Power of Guilt, Discouragement, and Defeat*

Kendra has inspired me once again with her winsome enthusiasm and encouragement. *Heart Clutter* has motivated me to keep clearing out and generously giving away. I'm only keeping what really matters, aiming to take her challenge to vigilantly keep my life clean.

♥**Dr. Catherine Hart Weber, Therapist. Life Coach.**
Author of *Flourish: Discover Vibrant Living*

In *Heart Clutter,* Kendra Smiley wraps real-life and often humorous stories around biblical principles. As she leads readers in looking at the emotional clutter of their hearts, she offers practical ways to analyze what needs to be tossed—such as false guilt, forgiven sins, hurt, and anger—and what needs to be shared with others or kept for personal growth. Journaling questions for quiet ponderings or group discussions encourage life-changing decisions.

♥**Sandra P. Aldrich, author of** *Heart Hugs for Single Moms: 52 Devotions to Encourage You*

HEART CLUTTER

HEART CLUTTER

SIFTING THROUGH THE CONTENTS OF
MY HEART, MIND, AND MEMORY.

KENDRA SMILEY

Bold Vision Books
PO Box 2011
Friendswood, Texas 77549

ISBN: 978-06-92389911

Published in the United States of America

Interior designed by *k*ae Creative Solutions
Cover design by *k*ae Creative Solutions

Cover Photo: Nikkizalewski / Dreamstime

Bold Vision Books
PO Box 2011
Friendswood, Texas 7759

DEDICATION

This book is dedicated to my husband John, a man who through the years has helped me determine what to Throw Away, what to Give Away, and what to Keep.

TABLE OF CONTENTS

Acknowledgments

When I read a book, I always start at the very beginning—even before the introduction and chapter one. I read the title page and the dedication and I never pass over the acknowledgments. I have always imagined the folks named in this section were the true heroes.

It is with love and a great big smile I thank my husband, John. He has provided inspiration and encouragement for this project and every other one I've ever tackled. A warm thanks to our sons, their wives, and the fun grandchildren John and I enjoy. I have been granted grace I don't deserve and given permission to share stories from their lives.

A big thank you to Karen Porter who has been my friend for many years and now wears an additional hat as a significant member of the publishing team.

And finally, thanks to the One who made this possible—Thank you, Lord.

Introduction

As the saying goes, in spring a young man's fancy turns to thoughts of love. Although I am not certain exactly what a "fancy" is, I think it is safe to admit that in spring my fancy turns to thoughts of clearing the clutter.

I want to be quick to point out two important things: I am never overly pleased by these thoughts; and it is not necessarily the season that precipitates them. I would hate to blame the lovely weather or harness it mercilessly to my anti-clutter urges. Occasionally these thoughts occur in the summer, fall, and winter too. More than the calendar, they are activated by an attack of overwhelming clutter in my life.

"The screwdriver is in the drawer by the refrigerator. If you don't see it right away, look under the coupon collection, the prolific pen and pencil pile, the warranties and the guarantees." That type of response is often heard in our household. That one and, "I know it's in there somewhere!"

Actually the words, "I know it's in there somewhere," are said more from hope than confidence and it is statements like that which many times have motivated me to consider cleaning out my drawers, shelves, and closets. I should note that step one—"considering" the task of uncluttering—is much more pleasant than actually doing the work. So is "thinking about" or "contemplating" the process.

Mom's Plan and My Heart

I do not come unprepared or untrained for the task of eliminating clutter and simplifying my life. When I was young, my mother made sure I developed skills to handle any possible accumulation of possessions. In fact, it was typical for my mom to enter my bedroom the very first day of summer vacation with three empty boxes and a big black marker. The boxes were never the same size. One was very large, one medium size, and the third one much smaller. Mom would announce that my job for the day (or for however long it took) was to sort through everything in my room, a project I fondly referred to as dejunking. At that point she would take her marker and label the largest box "Throw Away," the medium sized box "Give Away," and the smallest one "Keep." As a child I could never understand why Mom was not able to find three boxes closer to the same size. That fact did not seem to bother her in the least.

After the labeling was complete, I started the job. I went through every drawer, every shelf, and every hanger in the closet. Each item I handled had to go into a box. Throw Away, Give Away, or Keep. The plan was very simple and effective, yet it was always plagued by two serious problems. Actually they were two very serious and fundamental questions, questions that hovered over the dejunking and cast their dark shadows on the process.

Fundamental question number one: What if I throw this item away and then discover I need it? This is a terrifying prospect for many of you, especially if you are the self-appointed archivist for any particular group. Who will keep the old newsletters and minutes if you don't? Who will store the programs from past presentations and functions, the slips of paper too precious to destroy?

Or perhaps you maintain the official warehouse for Vacation Bible School paraphernalia. Who will stockpile the used Popsicle sticks and the frozen orange juice can lids if you don't? What if you throw these things away and you or anyone else in a four-county area discovers you need them? These are challenging questions that make cleaning the clutter more difficult.

On to fundamental question number two which is equally tough to answer: What if I keep this item and it is only junk? I know that thought has occurred to many of you. If you choose to keep it, you will continue tripping over the clutter until you dejunk again. And if you are a skilled procrastinator or have extensive storage, it might be years before you face that particular piece of clutter again.

Those two dilemmas always complicated the process of cleaning my room. They did not, however, keep me from doing it. Mom made sure of that. Early each summer during my growing up years, for as far back as I can remember, I started and completed the task.

Eventually I was married and no longer had the responsibility of clearing the clutter from my childhood bedroom. Now I had more shelves, drawers, cubbyholes, and closets than ever before. I had more places to store things, some not used or even useful. As distasteful and demanding as I might have felt my mother's system was, I found myself using precisely the same routine. One day several years ago as I began the process of determining what I should throw away, give away and keep, my mind began to wander.

CLEARING THE HEART CLUTTER

I began to wonder if I could use Mom's system to clear the clutter in my heart. Could I empty the contents of my heart, mind, and memory and sort through the clutter? Were there things I could throw away? Did I have anything inside of me to give away? Anything I should keep?

The longer I pondered the idea the more I realized Mom's plan had great potential for dejunking not only the drawer by the refrigerator but also my life. For years my home had benefited from her system and I was beginning to believe the drawers, shelves, and cubbyholes of my heart, mind, and memory could benefit from it too! So the process began, the process of sorting through what I had accumulated inside of me. I started sifting through the things I had been storing and putting each into the appropriate "box." Throw Away, Give Away, Keep – I began getting rid of the heart clutter I had accumulated.

Are you interested in doing the same? There is no need for boxes or a big black marker. Just imagine those boxes and choose to have a teachable spirit. Then turn the page and join me on the journey!

❤ *Kendra Smiley*

♥

1

CHOOSE TO THROW AWAY FALSE GUILT

Even though the box my mother had labeled "Throw Away" was the biggest of the three, I usually managed to fill it. When I started the task of removing the clutter from my heart, mind, and memory, I wondered if the same would prove true. Would I find more than one thing that needed to be thrown away? Upon examination, I realized the answer was a resounding "Yes." There were several things that definitely needed to go and one in particular was the guilt I had been harboring. You may be able to relate.

It is no wonder people talk about being on a guilt trip. The word picture is perfect.

Imagine the suitcases you have packed for trips in the past. Upon returning home you are faced with the job of unpacking, a chore I have never relished. It is tedious having to remove every item and return it to its place, not to mention having to wash loads of vacation laundry.

Now imagine the task of unpacking bags filled with guilt. Envision yourself examining each situation that has caused guilt, identifying the origin of the emotion, and determining where the guilt belongs. It's not easy, but much of that guilt might belong in the Throw Away box. The longer you travel with guilt, the more bags there will be to unpack.

The Power of One Small Word

I have had my share of guilt trips. They have been caused by a myriad of things, some noteworthy and others seemingly insignificant. Even the small word "no" can be a guilt producer.

Let's take a look at that little word. When you were a child it was probably one of your favorite answers to almost any question. It was a powerful weapon of control. I have known children who have chosen to say no when they really wanted to say "yes," simply to show they could!

"Do you want an ice cream cone?"

"No…well, maybe."

That conversation with a 2-year-old bent on dominance is not atypical. As an adult, however, things change. For whatever reason, something mysterious happens as we grow up. We find it more and more difficult to say no, especially when asked if we can do something that is considered good, kind, or charitable.

"Can you make another four dozen cookies for Teacher Appreciation Day?"

"Okay."

"Will you be on the decorating committee for the retreat?"

"All right."

"I need a substitute teacher for Sunday school. Can I count on you?"

"I suppose."

Adults seem to forget how to say no even though as a child it was their favorite word. I have decided this riddle is linked to the type of questions most adults are asked. People will rarely ask you to do something evil or unscrupulous.

When was the last time you heard the question, "Do you have time to do a dastardly deed?"

I can only hope you have never heard that question. It is more likely you are asked to do a good thing. So you say yes, motivated many times by guilt. It wouldn't be right to say no, would it?

Gina, a busy mother of four, had agreed to make forty vests for the children's Bible club. She said yes to a good thing, but later confided, "As I sat at my sewing machine making vests for other children I found myself screaming at my own kids." In hindsight, even though she might have had to deal with the guilt of saying no, perhaps that should have been her answer. Saying yes when no is the better reply is exactly how guilt becomes a prime source of clutter. Even though Gina dodged the bullet of guilt by saying yes to the request to make vests, she had to deal with the guilt of yelling at her own kids.

TWO KINDS OF GUILT

Having discussed the negative impact guilt has on our lives, I have to admit that not all guilt should be thrown away. It has been my experience there is bad guilt (bound for the Throw Away box) and good guilt (to be examined, handled, and eliminated by an admission of wrongdoing and a change in behavior). Bad guilt, also termed false guilt, results when there has been no intentional wrongdoing. Good

19

guilt, on the other hand, occurs when there has been a deliberate misbehavior or irresponsible act. It is the result of your conscience being alerted because your actions conflict with your knowledge of correct behavior. Good guilt must be handled differently than bad guilt.

These two varieties of guilt are not always easy to distinguish. Honesty is an indispensible tool in the identification process. When you discover the clutter of guilt in your heart, mind, or memory, the first step is to be truthful about the situation. "Then you will know the truth, and the truth will set you free" (John 8:32). If only being honest was always easy to *do*! Several years ago, I found myself in the difficult predicament of determining whether the guilt I was feeling was bad/false guilt to be cast into the Throw Away box, or good guilt capable of teaching me an important lesson?

Because we attend a small church, being a "no show" at a special event is something that can cause guilt. When there aren't many of you, it is easy to notice who is missing. One Saturday night, our church hosted a guest speaker but our family was not in attendance. My very legitimate excuse (said the woman sounding rather defensive) was that our eldest son was on the football team in college and he had a game that evening.

The following morning, at Sunday service, I inquired about the program and was informed it had been poorly attended. That report resulted in a load of guilt for me. I had to ask myself if I was feeling good guilt—something I could learn from—or bad guilt destined for the Throw Away box.

Before you jump to my defense and declare it bad guilt, I have to admit two things. First, our son had not yet attended enough

20

practices to be in uniform for the game. Second, I really did not want to hear the speaker. With those two pieces of information, you have probably completely shifted loyalties and are ready to assume I was experiencing good guilt.

The truth is actually twofold. True, I had no desire to attend the evening service and the football game was a legitimate excuse. But, beyond that, I was not personally responsible for the success or failure of the program. I had not committed to attending, and I had not encouraged the committee to select that specific date.

So what's the verdict on the guilt I was feeling? In this instance, I concluded it was bad guilt. I had not intentionally done anything wrong and for that reason I tossed the guilt into the Throw Away box.

THE GOODS ON GOOD GUILT

What happens when prayer leads you to determine your guilt is good guilt? Let's go back to that little word no.

My phone rang and it was a woman asking if I could teach a group of 5th and 6th graders for a week during a summer program. For whatever reason, I did not find it difficult to answer no. I determined she would not have a problem finding someone else to accept the position. She responded with a request I have heard on more than one occasion. "Would you mind praying about it?" She told me to take my time. She didn't need a commitment right away.

Too often, I've experienced the words " please pray about it" used as a guilt-fueler rather than a legitimate request. This woman, however, seemed to be making a genuine appeal, so I did just that—I prayed about it. As I spent time asking the Lord for direction, He revealed to me that there was good guilt associated with my negative answer. I was actually being selfish by thinking it must be someone else's turn. When, through prayer, I realized the truth, I called the woman back and agreed to teach the class. I had determined my guilt was good guilt and I chose to change my behavior.

What Gives Us Guilt?

Saying *no* is not the only thing that can produce guilt. "When the baby was born," one of my girlfriends once confided, "I got seven pounds of baby and fourteen pounds of guilt." According to her, guilt was standard issue and not an option. Maybe you can attest to that. I certainly experienced my share of guilt in motherhood, a task for which I was ill prepared.

I was the baby in my family and as a teenager I did very little babysitting. That is an understatement. Actually I can only remember one time. I was hired to watch the daughter of one of the high school coaches. The preschooler was sweet and well behaved and did not give me any problem. When I returned home that evening, however, I distinctly remember telling my mother there *had* to be an easier way to make money! As far as I was concerned, mowing lawns was a better job. Needless to say, my introduction to motherhood was quite a challenge.

After six years of marriage, I gave birth to our eldest son. I distinctly remember the experience of giving him his first bath. The poor kid almost froze to death. My mother and sister crowded into our bathroom and read me every step from the hospital instruction sheet. I wanted this momentous occasion to be perfect, but I became frazzled by everyone giving input, everyone telling me how I should bathe my son. Sadly, the "everyone" included my aunt who didn't even have

22

children! Their concern about my ineptness, combined with their expressions of pity for the baby, left me feeling very inadequate.

Do you think I experienced guilt? Absolutely! I didn't want to be the first woman in the family to inadvertently freeze her child to death during his first bath. By the end of that experience I was certain I was a terrible mom. Was I? No, I was simply an inexperienced one. I needed to persevere, learn, and gain experience. The good news is my eldest survived my early attempts at mothering a newborn. In turn, his younger brothers reaped the benefits of my practice. I stand on my record. I did not freeze one child!

"BUT MOM..."

Kids can serve up guilt very effectively when they discover it is a great source of motivation and manipulation.

"But Mom, *everyone* has a smart phone!"

"But Mom, I *need* these $175 tennis shoes!"

"Why can't I go to the Junior High party, Mom? Give me *one good reason.*"

Statements like those, in one form or another, have been effective guilt-producers for years. The question is: What kind of guilt is it? The answer lies in the truth of each statement. Let's examine them.

"But Mom, *everyone* has a smart phone." Come on now. When you hear the words *everyone, all, never,* or *always,* feel free to raise your eyebrows. Those words are seldom (Did you notice I didn't say *never?*) accurate. *Everyone* does not have a smart phone. That is the truth. No need to accept guilt when you hear exaggerations like that.

"But Mom, I *need* these $175 tennis shoes." There may be many things people *want,* but the truth is, there are very few things we *need.* Check the definition of the word need: to require (something) because it is essential or very important.

People need water, food, shelter, and basic clothing. No guilt for Mom in this comment either!

"Why can't I go to the Junior High party, Mom? Give me *one good reason.*" We actually heard this question from our oldest son. Kids grow up fast enough and my husband and I determined there was no reason to rush it. Feel free to call us old-fashioned (or the meanest parents on the block) if you must, but we decided our sons would not be allowed to attend coed parties while they were in junior high. School functions coupled with youth activities at church provided an adequate amount of socialization for our boys.

When this particular question was asked, we were able to provide more than *one good reason.* As you may have guessed, the list was not sufficient for the son who had raised the question. The debate that followed was controlled and unemotional. Even as we learned the party was only going to be "loosely" chaperoned, we kept our cool. Our son methodically countered each point we made with a seemingly persuasive rebuttal. The discussion finally came to a close when Dad posed a challenging question.

"I have a pretty good idea of what might happen at this loosely chaperoned party. Would you rather stay home or give us a call to get you when something inappropriate happens?"

After a long pause, our son's answer came: "Fine."

Translation? "Okay. Discussion over. I give up."

24

When the facts were presented and the decision was made, we felt no guilt about denying him the option of attending the party. The next morning at breakfast, the frustrated debater's younger brother spoke up. "Oh, by the way, when I'm in Junior High you won't need to give that boy-girl party speech. I heard the whole thing last night." Guilt level? Zero!

MOUTHS OF BABES

Unlike my previous example, there are times when it *is* possible to experience good guilt in relation to your kids and to learn a valuable lesson from it.

One day I received a phone call that totally preoccupied me for at least thirty minutes. When the conversation was over and I'd hung up, I walked into the living room and encountered a shocking surprise. Our toddler had taken every single toy out of the toy box and off the shelves and had scattered them all around the room.

Because he is our third child (Trust me, this does make a difference.), I had learned how to respond rather than react to situations such as this. I inhaled slowly and proceeded to give him some instruction in a calm voice. "You have made a real mess here. I want you to pick up all the toys and put them away."

His reply stunned me. "I'm too busy to pick up my toys *nanny* more times."

I took another deep breath and imagined I had not heard his reply. "What did you say?"

"I'm too busy," he repeated, oblivious to the imminent danger. "I'm not going to pick up my toys *nanny* more times."

At this point, I asked myself where he had gotten that belligerent attitude. When did Sesame Street start teaching the phrase, "I'm too busy?" Well, OK, maybe he didn't hear it on Sesame Street. Maybe, just maybe, he heard *me* say it once or twice.

Suddenly, I felt good guilt creeping in and I determined to begin resolving it immediately. With one more deep breath, the conversation continued. "Well, I can see how a guy like you might be too busy. I get busy sometimes. So I'll just pick up these toys for you and give them to some little boy who isn't as busy."

He looked up at me, obviously pondering his options. Then, after an instant of reflection, he replied, "You could give them to my brother cause he has to share with me!"

Pretty clever, huh? I want you to know I did not have to give the toys away to anyone, not even his brother, because the little guy ended up putting everything in the toy box. More importantly, I took a close look at my reasons for busyness and determined to make a concerted effort not to be "too busy" for the things that matter—like my precocious son.

AND ON IT GOES

Guilt-producing discussions don't stop at the toddler age, junior high, or even the adult stages of life. A woman in her seventies shared this memory with me. Her daughter had come to her with a complaint. In no uncertain terms, she brought to light some parental mistakes her mother had made decades before.

"When I was a cheerleader in high school you missed most of the games! Now as a mother, myself, I realize how important being there is and what a poor job you did!"

26

As the older woman told me the story, she admitted there were games she'd missed, but wondered why her daughter didn't remember when she'd taken the time to dye all the cheerleaders shoes or when she'd hosted the annual sleep-over. This poor mother was experiencing guilt and knew she would have to deal with the heart clutter in order to gain resolution and healing.

In like manner, unfortunately, parents are also capable of delivering guilt. Preparing to deplane after a trip, I overheard a conversation between two gentlemen in the seats behind me.

"I usually travel on Sunday or Monday, but I'm flying in a day early for this trip."

"Why is that?"

"To see my parents and do my yearly duty. Guilt, you know."

I have no idea why this man was reticent to visit his parents but he did share his motivation. It was guilt.

Family in every way, shape, and form, can be responsible for producing guilt. If it is false guilt it needs to be placed into the Throw Away box. Good guilt can be a positive motivator if the recipient is willing to admit the intentional or irresponsible behavior, ask for forgiveness, and make a change. Those actions will clear the clutter.

APOLOGY ACCEPTED?

When my children were very young they discovered the manipulative power of the words "I'm sorry." They learned that when I caught them in an offense, they could utter an apology and I would grant them an instant reprieve. That worked well *until* I realized they did not actually mean it when they said, "I'm sorry." How did I know that? Because their behavior had not changed. When it dawned on me that their regret was insincere, the jig was up.

"Quit chasing your brother."

"I'm sorry."

"No, you're not. This is the second time I've asked you. If you were sorry you would have stopped."

Saying "I'm sorry" means nothing without a change in behavior, a change in direction.

I'm Sorry For...

A while back, I ran into an acquaintance I had not seen in years. We sat down to enjoy a soft drink together and he began to pour out the recent events of his life. It was not a pretty picture.

His wife had kicked him out of their home, his children were estranged from him, and he was struggling to keep his job. Oh, yes, and he was having an affair. He explained that his troubles had started after his wife discovered his adultery. While releasing this barrage of information he kept saying, "I'm sorry. I'm just so sorry."

Finally I had heard more than enough of the gruesome details and I abruptly presented him with a question. "Are you sorry for committing adultery and losing your family or are you sorry for getting caught?"

It was obvious he had never thought about that before. After a moment or two he answered in complete honesty, "I guess I'm sorry I got caught."

28

If he was experiencing any guilt at all (and I'm not sure he was), it was good guilt. Good guilt could have pushed this man to admit his wrongdoing, ask for forgiveness, and change his behavior. The words of scripture are clear. "Let us draw near to God with a sincere heart and with the full assurance that faith brings, having our hearts sprinkled to cleanse us from a guilty conscience and having our bodies washed with pure water" (Hebrews 10:22).

REFLECTION

TIME TO CLEAR THE HEART CLUTTER

Ask the Lord to help you take an honest look into your heart, mind, and memory. Do you see any guilt? Take time to jot down anything the Holy Spirit brings to mind. You don't need to write a full explanation, just a word or two to remind you of the incidence, words, or thoughts.

Next, ask yourself: What is the truth about each situation? You might want to focus on one thing for several days. As God reveals the truth to you through the Word or His still, small voice, take note. John 8:32 is clear. It is this truth that will set you free.

Finally, in light of the truth, determine if it is good guilt or bad guilt. If it's bad guilt, throw it away. You might want to literally do just that by writing down the bad guilt on a piece of paper and disposing of it. If it's good guilt, take the following steps:

1. Admit your wrongdoing and ask forgiveness. This might be something done privately between you and the Lord. Or maybe He's asking you to include others. Follow whatever instruction the Lord is giving you.

2. Change your behavior. Instead of making a public announcement, let your actions do the talking. The change will be obvious after a time.

3. Accept the forgiveness God extends to you. If this is difficult for you to do, take heart and read on. It is the emphasis of the next chapter.

♥

2

CHOOSE TO THROW AWAY FORGIVEN SINS

Guilt is not the only thing I discovered while sifting through the clutter in my heart, mind, and memory. I uncovered a stockpile of forgiven sins, sins I had repented of and for which I had received forgiveness. There they were, stored in my heart in an unhealthy way. I could not seem to forget my wrongdoing.

When I sin—"for all have sinned and fall short of the glory of God" (Romans 3:23)—I can choose to admit my wrongdoing and ask God to forgive me. I know what the Word says about forgiveness. "If we confess our sins, he is faithful and just and will forgive us our sins and purify us from all unrighteousness" (1 John 1:9).

God is more than willing to forgive me when I truly repent. The problem is, I don't always forgive myself. This means days, maybe weeks later, I remember those sins and, in remorse, ask for forgiveness again. But, the Bible says God forgives *and* forgets. "I, even I, am he who blots out your transgressions, for my own sake, and remembers your sins no more" (Isaiah 43:25).

I imagine the conversation going something like this: "Lord, I'm sorry for what I did. I know I've asked you before, but I'm asking again. Please forgive me."

"Kendra, I have no recollection of what you are talking about."

He doesn't remember because He has already extended forgiveness and remembers my sin no more.

SHOP TALK

Forgiveness is yours because Christ has already paid for your sins. When I think about the concept of paying, shopping comes to mind. Here's an interesting scenario for you to ponder. A woman entered a small boutique and immediately noticed the rack marked "Clearance." She rummaged through the clothing, spotting an adorable skirt just her size along with a blouse and sweater. She scurried into the tiny dressing room where, in solitude, she determined whether or not the ensemble was attractive. She then calculated the discount to determine if the items were really a bargain. It was a good shopping day! Everything fit and the prices were definitely right.

With more than a hint of satisfaction, she took her purchases to the register clerk. Using a very old fashioned system, the shopkeeper listed each piece of clothing on a carbon-backed receipt: one skirt, one blouse, one sweater. The items were totaled and the shopper paid cash for the exact amount of the sale. In return, she received a copy of the receipt with the words "Paid in Full" written across the bottom.

What she owed was taken care of by the exchange of money. What we owe for our sins is taken care of and paid in full by Jesus Christ's sacrifice on the cross. Unlike the receipt that gave an account of all the items the woman had purchased, when Christ paid our debt, our sins were no longer listed. There are no carbon copies, no reminders of the debt that has been paid.

You would think, with this knowledge, it would be as easy as pie to accept forgiveness, but I still struggle. More than once I have made

32

a mistake, asked for forgiveness, and then had difficulty accepting forgiveness from God or from the one I offended

JUST DESSERT

John and I had been teaching a Bible study on marriage. On the evening of one of our meetings, all of the couples in the group went out for dinner and then stopped at a local ice cream shop for dessert. The women sat at the picnic tables while the men went up to the window to order. To my dismay, when John handed me my sweet treat, I saw that it was not what I had requested. For whatever reason, I decided that it was a big deal. Rather than eat what was delivered, I reacted poorly, telling him in a quiet, disappointed voice that he had not gotten my order right. As quickly as the words slipped out of my mouth, I realized how inappropriate they were. Unfortunately, trying to stuff them back into my mouth would have been as difficult as attempting to push toothpaste back into the toothpaste tube. I quickly apologized, and accepted the delicacy he had offered.

John seemed to have no problem accepting my apology and went on to visit with the other couples. I, on the other hand, was miserable. I was ashamed of my self-centered behavior and pride, and I inwardly declared myself the least qualified to teach others about marriage. While waging this war within myself, I noticed that no one else seemed to care. The mood of the party suffered no dark cloud. I was the only one experiencing a sudden damper on the evening.

When we got home I apologized, again, but John reassured me it was no big deal. I also asked God to forgive me for my arrogant attitude and pride. My repentance was genuine. The next morning, however, I felt just as miserable as I had the night before. "How could God forgive me? He expects more from me as a teacher. I know I've let him down."

In the midst of my self-pity party, the phone rang. Sharon, a long distance friend of mine, was on the line. She and I had not talked for almost four years, but we always exchanged cards and letters at Christmas to stay in touch. "Hi, Kendra. This is Sharon. I know you must be surprised to hear from me."

"I sure am, but what a treat! What's new?"

"Well, this morning in my prayer time you came to mind so I prayed for you. Then the strangest thing happened. I knew God wanted me to call you with a message."

As soon as she said that I grabbed a pen and a pad of paper. I knew Sharon well and had observed her walk with Christ for many years. She was not someone to deliver a contrived message. If Sharon had a message for me from God, I wanted to get it all down.

"He wanted me to tell you He loves you. Isn't that wild? I know you know that but I couldn't get it out of my mind. I was supposed to call you so I did. That's it."

"Thanks, Sharon. That was just the message I needed to hear!" She had no idea what I had been thinking. She had no reason to believe I had doubted God's love for me. She didn't know a thing about my poor behavior at the ice cream shop the night before. What she did know was that on occasion God speaks to us, quietly, so that his message can only be heard by listening with your heart. She also knew that at times the message is for someone else. In this case that "someone" was me. On that day I was thankful for Sharon's obedience and for reassurance of the overwhelming fact that God loves me. He knew my heart, had forgiven me, and was willing to help me forgive myself. He knows your heart, has forgiven you each time you repent, and will help you forgive yourself.

34

The Cross is Central

Jenny had been asked to communicate God's message of repentance and forgiveness at a women's retreat. In preparation, she constructed a life-sized cross, which she used as a focal point. She spoke on the reality of sin, the importance of repentance, and our guaranteed victory over sin because of Christ's sacrifice. "Ladies, this cross is empty. Jesus left the cross in order to make room for our sins. Now we must choose to admit our sins, repent, and nail them to that cross."

After that admonishment, she provided paper, pens, nails, and a hammer, encouraging her audience to prayerfully give their burdens to Christ. Once the women had penned their confessions, they were to literally nail them to the cross as a symbol of release. The expectancy was that the former owner would not be reclaiming these written burdens. They now belonged in the Throw Away box.

God in a Box

Perhaps my difficulty in accepting God's forgiveness stems from my knowledge that I am not as generous about extending forgiveness. I try to squeeze God into a human-sized box so I can understand Him better, thus, attempting to limit Him as I am limited. However, my attempts are in vain because God is not limited to my knowledge or nature. "My thoughts are not your thoughts, neither are your ways my ways," declares the Lord. 'As the heavens are higher than the earth, so are my ways higher than your ways and my thoughts than your thoughts."[1]

Try restricting God to a box and He'll explode from it every time! He is incapable of being defined because He has no limits. His sovereignty means He can do anything He wants to do with or without us. Psalm

115:3 reads, "Our God is in heaven; he does whatever pleases him", and it pleases him to forgive us when we repent. That is why even when it is difficult for me, I can look to His example of unconditional pardon and pray to be more like Him.

REFLECTION

TIME TO CLEAR THE HEART CLUTTER

"Or do you not know that wrongdoers will not inherit the kingdom of God? Do not be deceived: Neither the sexually immoral nor idolaters nor adulterers nor men who have sex with men nor thieves nor the greedy nor drunkards nor slanderers nor swindlers will inherit the kingdom of God. And that is what some of you were. But you were washed, you were sanctified, you were justified in the name of the Lord Jesus Christ and by the Spirit of our God" (1 Corinthians 6:9-11).

Take a moment to think back on forgiven sins that might be cluttering your heart, mind, or memory, and make a note of them in the space below. After each offense is noted, write this verse: "I, even I, am he who blots out your transgressions, for my own sake, and remembers your sins no more" (Isaiah 43:25).

Commit the verse to memory and recite it whenever you are tempted to forget this promise of God.

♥

3

CHOOSE TO THROW AWAY
HURTS AND DISAPPOINTMENTS

My virtual Throw Away box was filling up, rapidly. Good thing it was the biggest one! Still, I suspected there were a few more items of clutter that needed to go. Upon further inspection, I found several hurts in my heart. I had allowed them a place to hide for far too long.

HURTS OF ALL SIZES

Hurts can take a variety of shapes and forms. They can be fresh and new or almost as old as you are. Not everyone reacts to a hurt in the same way; a hurt that is bearable to one individual may prove overwhelming to another. Despite this diversity, they do have one thing in common. These nasty bits of clutter all cause pain and it can be hard to heal and move on when you allow them to rest in your heart, mind, or memory.

A talented group of women invited me to join a team of speakers at a three-day event. I had fun spending time getting to know them as individuals and one of my favorites was Brenda, a single mother. We enjoyed each other's company while exchanging stories of the pleasures and perils of motherhood, especially as mothers of boys. We commented on how we frequently vacillated between the positions of "princess" and "maid," with the emphasis on "maid."

On the second day of the conference, Brenda received a disturbing voicemail from a good friend. Days earlier, before leaving home, Brenda had made carpooling arrangements with this friend to transport her son to a special sporting event. In the phone message the woman explained that something unexpected had come up and she would not be able to give Brenda's son a ride. My friend, who was many miles from her home, listened in disbelief. This woman had changed her plans at the last minute. Couldn't she have found someone else to fill in for her?

Emotions were high as Brenda told me of the situation, and I immediately went into problem-solving mode. Obviously, it was not a life or death situation, but with no one else to fill the gap, creativity was needed. I had offered several suggestions when I realized Brenda was not giving any input or putting forth any effort to help resolve the issue. I paused, giving her my full attention, and she quietly spoke. "Why would my friend do something like this? She knew it would hurt me."

She was more conflicted with feelings of hurt and disappointment than the seemingly obvious need to determine a Plan B for her son. Brenda was crushed by the sudden change of plans and felt it was a betrayal of friendship and a purposeful assault on their relationship.

Brenda's friend may not have realized how upsetting this would be, but it really didn't matter whether the hurt was intentional or unintentional. Brenda's perception was that this friend had served her a big disappointment, and it was quickly settling into her heart. As I observed my friend's reaction, I was prompted to pray, knowing that it wouldn't be long before she would need to sort through the clutter and put that hurt where it belonged—in the Throw Away box.

It Doesn't Really Matter

It is possible that some of the hurts, cluttering your heart are petty. If you choose to give them the space, they will stay there, content to keep you discontent.

I remember standing up in the bleachers after a very disappointing Little League game. Even though it was years ago, the lesson I learned that day has stayed with me. My youngest son played a good game, as had many of the other boys on the team. Unfortunately, the other team played just a little bit better.

"The kids did such a good job. If only they could have had another inning to catch up. I think they could have won the game," I complained. I continued to lament the outcome of the game, until one of my older sons, who had been sitting with me, decided I had whined long enough.

"Mom, you have to keep this in perspective. Is anyone going to hell because our team lost? If the answer to that question is no, it isn't all that important."

Hmmm… He was right, and since he'd managed to ask me the question in a relatively kind and loving way, I decided to grow with it rather than feeling hurt. Perspective *is* important.

Welcome In

As ridiculous as it may sound, I have actually *invited* hurts into my life. No, I didn't send out a formal invitation, but I did structure the situation so that the hurt would hit me right in the middle of my heart. I know this seems crazy, so let me give you an example.

40

Through the years, my friend Sue (an excellent pianist) and I collaborated on many children's musical programs in our church. My musical ability didn't compare to hers, but I made up for my lack of talent with enthusiasm. After one particularly delightful performance, I exuberantly connected with the first adult I saw walking toward the piano. "Wasn't that wonderful?" My question was bubbling with genuine appreciation for the talents and abilities of the children.

"Well, I didn't really like the middle part. I thought it was rather slow and boring."

Seriously? I wanted to scream! How could anyone not see how adorable those children were in *every* part! I bit my tongue as I considered the several ways I wanted to react to her negative evaluation. Fortunately, I simply nodded my head, in no particular direction and the woman wandered off.

I had brought that hurtful encounter upon myself. I had gone fishing for a compliment and instead caught hurt and disappointment. I had to make a choice. Would I allow those words to find a place in my heart, mind, and memory? Or would I relax and make myself a promise or two? First promise: to realize the benefit of visualizing a "No Fishing" sign when it came to compliments. Second: to continue giving out compliments to others even if they are fishing for them.

Keeping Score

If you are a mother, you know that your opportunity to experience hurts and disappointments is mathematically proportionate to the number of children you have—the more kids, the more possibilities. It's my theory that the umbilical cord is never actually cut. It just stretches a *really* long way!

As a relatively stable adult, I was baffled when it dawned on me that my heart had collected not simply my own hurts, but those of my children. I learned that these hurts needed frequent attention to keep clutter from accumulating. Children seem to be able to forgive more quickly than their mothers. Moms tend to keep score; kids tear up the scorecards.

SO AND SO DID SUCH AND SUCH

When I was asked to solicit help for a community function I had no idea what I would learn. My job was to contact a list of people and see if they would be willing to help in a certain capacity. One of my calls proved quite intriguing.

"Hi, my name is Kendra Smiley, and I was given your name as someone who might be willing to serve on the kitchen committee for the upcoming event."

"Who else in on the committee?" That seemed to be a strange question, one I hadn't been asked by anyone else. I proceeded to read her the list and when I got to one particular name, I was abruptly interrupted. "I'm sorry but I can't be on the committee if so-and-so is on it. You see, thirty years ago so-and-so did such-and-such."

I marveled at this woman's memory, but then it hit me. Her remembering the such-and-such that so-and-so had done thirty years ago was not a good thing. That ugly memory belonged in the Throw Away box instead of adding clutter to her heart.

ONE BAD WEEK

Hurts don't have to be stored for thirty years to be damaging. One bad week can get the job done, too. Consider Linda and her husband Tom.

On Monday, Tom did not roll the garbage containers to the curb. On Tuesday, he forgot to stop and pick up milk on his way home from work. On Wednesday, he announced to his wife that on Thursday he was responsible for bringing cookies for the monthly office-wide coffee break. ("Gee Honey, didn't I mention that before?) On Thursday, he told Linda he was going to play golf on Saturday so she'd have the three preschoolers to herself.

All week long Linda silently harbored those disappointments. She smiled like a saint and was quite agreeable until Friday came. Friday, Tim called to tell Linda to cancel the babysitter. They would have to postpone their evening out because his boss needed him to pick up a package across town.

That was it! Linda had been teetering on the edge and this final let down had pushed her over. "What do you mean you *have* to pick up a package?! We have a babysitter coming and we've been planning an evening together!"

The explosion was a complete shock to clueless Tom, but before he could catch his breath and respond, Linda was already unloading the remaining clutter that had accumulated throughout the week. "And I'm sick of you playing golf! You can bake your own cookies next time. I'm obviously not important to you. You can't even remember to pick up milk or take out the garbage!"

By this time, poor Tim was desperately struggling to get his bearings. What did milk and cookies have to do with the package he had to retrieve? And where in the world did the garbage fit in?

THROW AWAY THE SCORE CARD

Why oh why are women such accomplished scorekeepers? It's not healthy and it's not profitable. Even so, chances are, like Linda, you've

43

got scorecards full of logged hurts (real or imagined). The annoyances caused by Tim had a mild impact when they occurred one by one. But when they piled up there was an explosion. Had Linda examined each one as they came, resolving the hurt and discarding it to the appropriate "box," the final blow out might have been avoided. The fact of the matter is that, on any particular afternoon, most people don't remember what they had for lunch much less how they may have inadvertently hurt or disappointed someone earlier in the week.

God's word specifically says love "keeps no record of wrongs."[2] Love doesn't keep score by accumulating and logging the hurts we experience in life. Instead, love resolves those grievances. Whether they're intentional or not, real or imagined, big or small, work through them and move on.

"Bear with each other and forgive whatever grievances you may have against one another. Forgive as the Lord forgave you" (Colossians 3:13).

REFLECTION

TIME TO CLEAR THE HEART CLUTTER

Look into your heart, mind, and memory, and locate the hurts and disappointments you are storing there. Write them down in the space below. Choose to let go of them, taking away their power over your actions and decisions, and your words.

Be certain you aren't holding on to hurts that are not even yours. Sometimes, we keep track of negative pieces of history for someone else. Jot these down and toss them away.

♥

4

CHOOSE TO THROW AWAY ARROGANCE AND SELFISHNESS

Sorting and sifting was wearing me out! Even though I was making significant progress, I was just about ready to quit. Was it possible I had found everything in my heart, mind, or memory that needed to be sentenced to the Throw Away box?

No such luck! I soon discovered a hidden pile of clutter that I needed to conquer. It had been shoved deep down and was pretty nasty. It reminded me of the remnant of a peanut butter sandwich I had stashed with my comic books when I was in elementary school. I came across that moldy surprise while dejunking my room one summer. The discovery was disgusting enough to make me want to ditch the job on the spot. At the same time, it reminded me how absolutely necessary it was to continue the process of ridding my room (and, later, my heart, mind, and memory) of forgotten messes. There was no moldy PB&J in my heart, but what I uncovered was just as disgusting. Things like arrogance and selfishness forced me to take a step back and realign myself with God's word.

PUZZLING PRIDE

Arrogance, or pride, can rear its ugly head when there has been no particular performance worthy of prideful feelings. I have been guilty of assuming the posture of pride to try and convince myself, and the world around me, that I have done something terrific. God's word is very specific, when it comes to this type of attitude, in Philippians 2:3:"Do nothing out of selfish ambition or vain conceit." These two things usually motivate an arrogant, conceited person.

I remember the first time that verse shouted at me. It seemed to jump off the page and I was immediately convicted by it. *Don't you just love it when God's word specifically identifies one of your shortcomings?* If your honest answer is no, I completely understand. I cannot say I have always classified those moments as wonderful, but I know that that God loves me, and His ord is true.

"No discipline seems pleasant at the time, but painful. Later on, however, it produces a harvest of righteousness and peace for those who have been trained by it" (Hebrews 12:11).

Because my goal was, and is, to be trained by God's discipline and His word, I knew I had to carefully examine myself in light of the Scripture "Do nothing out of selfish ambition or vain conceit."[3] Prior to reading those words on that fateful morning, I had volunteered for a project with both of those negative motivations in mind. I had managed to "Do something out of *both* selfish ambition *and* vain conceit."

My arrogance and pride, my selfish ambition and vain conceit, belonged in the Throw Away box. Having acknowledged those ulterior motives, I was determined to get rid of them. I repented, asking God for forgiveness and told Him I was willing to forgo the project I had undertaken for my own gain.

God knew my heart and saw my repentant attitude. Through a series of extraordinary events, he arranged for me to continue. Each time I worked with the group, I would silently remind myself that *nothing* was to be done from selfish ambition or vain conceit. *Nothing* was to be done in arrogance or pride. Before long, my attitude toward the assignment had genuinely changed and I began to serve rather than expecting to be served.

When the project was complete, God opened another door of opportunity for me. It doesn't always happen so quickly, but it *is* more likely to happen when you put aside selfish ambition and vain conceit and follow the Lord's instruction.

"Do nothing out of selfish ambition or vain conceit" (Philippians 2:3).

UP IN THE AIR

My husband John entered pilot training for the United States Air Force seven days after we were married, and a year later he received his wings. He flew and served on active duty for a few years. After leaving the cockpit, he put his college degree to work teaching math and became part of an Air Force Reserve Unit. Even though he wanted to fly again there were no flying positions available so he became the Intelligence Officer.

Each month on his Reserve weekend, he would inquire about the possibility of moving to a flying position but nothing changed. His talent, ambition, and persistence were not enough to make it happen. On one particular Reserve weekend he decided to spend his travel time to the Base praying specifically about his desire to fly. The culmination of his conversation with the Lord was the relinquishment of his dream of ever flying again. "I want what you want, Lord. If it is Your will that I never fly again, then that is what I want, too. I give

48

You my flying. I don't want it or anything else more than I want Your will in my life."

When John arrived at the base that day, the group commander greeted him. After a short conversation the commander miraculously asked my husband if he was still interested in flying. Yes, he was, and fly he did! He flew in the cockpit of a KC-135 for the next twenty plus years. John genuinely asked for God's will to be done and God chose to open a door of opportunity for him to fly. There was no selfish ambition and vain conceit. Those two motives belong in the Throw Away box!

It's Your Call

"It's for you Kendra." John handed me the phone and went into the other room.

"We have made our decision about the teaching position and we have decided to hire another applicant."

"Thank you. I appreciate your call." I hung up the phone and cried. And cried and cried and cried. How awful! I didn't get the job. I found it hard to believe the other candidate was more qualified. What could I do now? I didn't want to substitute teach. I wanted to have my own classroom. I deserved my own classroom.

Did you detect any arrogance in my attitude? I know your answer to that question and thankfully, I noticed it too. Now my job was to respond as God's word instructs. I pitched my arrogance into the Throw Away box and resolutely signed up to be a substitute teacher.

Before long, I was a regular on the local junior high campus. Five weeks into the school year, the junior high girls' physical education teacher, who had become my lunch buddy, posed an interesting question. "Are you still looking for a job?"

"Well, I've actually stopped actively looking because five weeks of school have already passed. But I am still interested."

"Did you know there is an opening in Potomac?"

"I don't even know where Potomac is."

"It's not too far from here and I know they're looking for a fourth grade teacher."

"That's terrific! Do you think I can get an interview?"

"I know you can! The principal is my brother."

Off we trotted to the junior high school office where she called her brother and arranged for my interview. That evening, I met the principal and several members of the school board, and by midnight I had the job! With the guidance found in God's Word I chose to make an attitude adjustment and God chose to provide another opportunity for me. Does it always happen just like that? No, but it is more likely to happen when you put aside selfish ambition and vain conceit and follow the Lord's instruction.

Reminder: "Do nothing out of selfish ambition or vain conceit" (Philippians 2:3).

You always have a choice. If you choose to operate in pride, selfish ambition, and vain conceit you are choosing disobedience. Sadly, I know that truth from experience. Selfish ambition and vain conceit belong in the Throw Away box.

OPERATING IN DISOBEDIENCE

The little church where I worship has been the location for many life-changing lessons. God used Cliff, a very large, mentally challenged young man, to teach me one of those lessons—another reminder of the importance of throwing away arrogant clutter.

Shortly after he moved to town, Cliff began showing up at church every Sunday. He did not actually come into the sanctuary but would stand outside the door, in the yard, or on the steps. At first no one was able to coax him inside. But after some time had passed he developed a friendship with our pastor and began to feel more comfortable, comfortable enough to join us inside.

Every Sunday, Cliff would arrive at eight o'clock for the 10 o'clock service. That was the time the praise team assembled to rehearse. His friend, our pastor, was a part of that group. As the praise team practiced, Cliff would wander through the sanctuary.

Aside from the pastor, there were two other guitarists, a pianist, and two primary vocalists. Linda sang soprano and had a beautiful voice, and I, once again compensating with enthusiasm, sang alto. In addition to singing, I was responsible for manipulating the transparencies on the overhead projector. If you're scratching your head and wondering what a transparency or an overhead projector might be, just imagine the precursor to power point slides and a projector. Remember, it was a small church with a small budget and at the time there were no personal computers to be had.

One morning as we played through the songs in our early morning rehearsal, Cliff became fascinated with the projector. He sat right beside it with his legs hanging over the raised platform, watching as

I changed the transparencies each time we started a new song. After several weeks of this, Cliff asked me if he could help. "Sure" was my reply and I handed him the next transparency. After each song Cliff gave me the one that had been on the screen and I handed him a new one. When our rehearsal ended Cliff resumed his wandering, ultimately settling in a pew in the most remote corner of the church to enjoy the rest of the morning.

Sunday after Sunday Cliff manipulated the overheads as the praise team practiced. Before long, he was taking all the songs for the morning and laying them in order on the altar rail. He was becoming quite adept at putting each one on the screen at the correct time. One Sunday, after practice, I asked Cliff if he would like to help during the worship service. His face lit up and he readily accepted the task. That was the day Cliff became the official "worship song transparency man." As he sat with his legs dangling over the podium, he did an impeccable job aiding the congregation in worship each week.

When the pastor called for the congregation to greet one another after the time of worship, Cliff would turn off the projector, shake my hand, and find his way to the most remote corner of the church. This went on for a many weeks. One Sunday, as the congregation greeted one another and the praise team disassembled, Cliff went to sit in a *different* pew this time—mine.

Please do not act shocked to hearing me call it "my pew." I'm certain most of you have "your pew," too, or your chair, or your favorite section of the sanctuary where you worship. My pew was where my family sat each week. Many times teenagers whose parents didn't attend church joined us, as did the occasional visitor. My pew was in the second row, so on that particular Sunday Cliff literally moved from the spot farthest from the lectern to the closest spot.

My first thought was, "Wait a minute. You're taking up a lot of space I might need." Thank goodness, instead of acting on that first thought, I simply slid in beside him and the service continued. I am sure the sermon that morning was probably pretty good, but I really do not remember. I spent most of the time cleaning out the ugly arrogance that had crept into my heart. It had to go into the Throw Away box, and the sooner, the better!

Up to that point, knowing Cliff had not inconvenienced me or made me feel uncomfortable. It had been easy to be kind in those former circumstances, but now Cliff was invading my space. I decided that I would be pleasant but do nothing to encourage his relocation. As I momentarily pondered that strategy, I ran headlong into my prideful feelings and I was ashamed. Once, again, I asked the Lord for forgiveness for my haughty spirit. I knew He wanted me to throw away my vain conceit and give away encouragement instead. The choice of obedience or disobedience was simple, but not necessarily easy. The sermon ended and the pastor opened up the service for the sharing of joys and concerns. I immediately knew what God wanted me to do.

"Pastor? I am thankful for Cliff's help during praise and worship time. He does a great job!"

I turned to look at Cliff and he was smiling from ear to ear and it seemed I had gained a permanent pew partner. So be it! Hanging on to pride and arrogance is never the best choice.

"For by the grace given me I say to every one of you: Do not think of yourself more highly than you ought, but rather think of yourself with sober judgment, in accordance with the faith God has distributed to each of you" (Romans 12:3).

Selfish Ambition in Ages Past

"Now the whole world had one language and a common speech. As people moved eastward, they found a plain in Shinar and settled there. They said to each other, "Come, let's make bricks and bake them thoroughly." They used brick instead of stone, and tar for mortar. Then they said, "Come, let us build ourselves a city, with a tower that reaches to the heavens, so that we may make a name for ourselves; otherwise we will be scattered over the face of the whole earth." But the Lord came down to see the city and the tower the people were building. The Lord said, "If as one people speaking the same language they have begun to do this, then nothing they plan to do will be impossible for them. Come, let us go down and confuse their language so they will not understand each other." So the Lord scattered them from there over all the earth, and they stopped building the city. That is why it was called Babel—because there the Lord confused the language of the whole world. From there the Lord scattered them over the face of the whole earth" (Genesis 11:1-9).

These folks wanted to make a name for themselves. They were motivated by selfish ambition, vain conceit, and aspirations that were and are not pleasing to God. I wonder what might have happened if they had abandoned their arrogant building project and put those attitudes into the Throw Away box. We will never know.

Reflection

♥

Time to Clear the Heart Clutter

Take another look at the clutter in your heart. Identify your motivations. Do you spot arrogance or selfish ambition in any area of your life? Write down what you discover and then put it into the Throw Away box.

Many times we are most selfish in our closest relationships. Can you identify any selfishness that may have infiltrated your deepest friendships? How about your relationship with your husband? Are you demanding and controlling when it comes to your friends and family? Be honest as you reflect on these questions and record your answers. Close your eyes and listen to the voice of God's spirit. As painful as it is to uncover arrogance and selfishness, it is more destructive to ignore those attitudes and allow them a place in your heart, mind, or memory.

5

CHOOSE TO THROW AWAY ANGER

Your Throw Away box might be getting pretty full. That's OK! As full as it is, you could still be housing more clutter that needs to be tossed. Believe it or not, I found more in my heart. I had thrown away false guilt, forgiven sins, hurts and disappointments, arrogance and selfishness, but I still needed to evict some anger that had been hiding deep inside.

Anger? *Moi?* As much as I wanted to deny it, the truth was that anger had found a place in my heart. You might find it interesting to know there was a time in my life when I would have wholeheartedly and sincerely denied the possibility I had any anger issues. After all, I never hit or kicked things and I was never guilty of throwing something at another person. Those were the signs of anger, weren't they? I was certain that was the case and declared myself anger-free.

BOWLS AND WORDS

Some time back, I was acquainted with a woman who, in my opinion, had a definite problem with anger. In contrast to me, she *did* throw things. In fact, in a fit of rage, she once threw an "unbreakable" bowl at her husband. He ducked and it missed him, but it hit the brick fireplace and shattered. The story goes that she had the audacity to send the pieces of the bowl to the manufacturer and ask for a replacement. After all, it was supposed to be unbreakable, wasn't it? Yes, under normal use. I guess she considered throwing a bowl at your husband "normal use."

"Like a city whose walls are broken through is a person who lacks self-control" (Proverbs 25:28).

That woman was angry. No doubt about it. But was it really possible I had anger cluttering? Sadly, the answer was yes. The difference between the agitated bowl buster and me was I had learned to express my anger in a socially acceptable manner. The anger inside of me was not evidenced by flying place settings but by flying sarcasm. Truthfully, I am not certain which of the assaults can do more damage, the physical one or a the more subtle verbal attack.

As a young child I found sarcasm to be a safe way to express my anger. I was angry about many things. I was angry that my father was a functional alcoholic. I was angry that our family chose to ignore the issue. I was angry that this carefully hidden curse seemed to dominate my life. Because the overt signs of anger were not tolerated in our home, I was forced to stifle those reactions and, instead I chose to spew forth sarcasm. Today, as a Christian, I realize sarcasm is a very destructive form of anger and has no place in my interactions. It belongs in the Throw Away box.

It is possible you have been the recipient of someone else's anger disguised by a mask of sarcasm. This can be confusing and hurtful. I vividly remember my own experience with just such a person from my early years as a speaker.

Sarcasm Coming Your Way

In any given professional field, there are people you come to admire, mostly from afar. That was the case with a particular keynote speaker I had the pleasure of hearing her when she addressed the audience of a large conference I attended. A few months later, I saw her at a smaller event and was looking forward to meeting her. Upon being officially introduced, I was both excited and intimidated. "It is such a treat to meet you. I heard your opening message at a Christian college recently and I really appreciated your words. I was unable to stay into the afternoon so I missed your second session."

As soon as those words were out of my mouth I regretted saying them. No speaker wants to hear that his or her message was preempted by something else. My genuine compliment had turned sour with the addition of the last sentence.

Unfortunately, she chose to react to the closing sentence rather than the opening, encouraging remarks. "You left before I spoke again? That's good to know. I'll have to see if I can attend a workshop on healing at the conference today."

Ouch! I got the point. My insensitive words had been rewarded by anger clothed in sarcasm. I suffered only a flesh wound and the recovery didn't take long, but the lesson was loud and clear: Despite what you witnessed today, Kendra, don't allow *your* sarcasm to wound someone else.

The Sullen Approach

Have you ever thought of yourself as an angry person? Maybe, like me, you have learned to express anger in a socially acceptable manner.

If sarcasm is not your weapon of choice, perhaps it is sullenness. A pouter seldom gets tagged with the angry label, but that kind of behavior might be an indicator there is anger in the clutter. I once heard a radio commentator declare that anger invisibly chains the angry person to the one with whom he is angry. That sounds a lot like what I used to tell our youngest son.

When he was growing up, before he became taller than both his older brothers, they took pleasure in teasing him. It was nothing serious or mean, but they enjoyed seeing if they could get him to react. My response was always the same: "The big boys are just trying to pull your chain. All you have to do is ignore them and they'll stop."

Although it might have been easier to ignore me than to ignore his brothers, the advice was correct. They were able to make him react because of his anger. He was the marionette and they were the puppeteers.

That same principle applies to adults. Image you are out on a Saturday morning running errands and doing a little shopping. It is almost noon so you decide to treat yourself to your favorite sandwich at your favorite fast food restaurant. As you pull into the parking lot, lo and behold, there is *Her* car. (Feel free to fill in the appropriate name.) *She* is inside and you really don't want to see her! What do you do? You pull through the parking lot and head for a different restaurant and a different sandwich. You drive down the street and settle for your second or third favorite sandwich. Who won? Who was in charge? Who got to eat the best sandwich?

Everyone has feelings of anger. Acting on those feelings by violent action, sarcasm, pouting, or any other behavior done with the desire to hurt another person is a sin.

"In your anger do not sin": Do not let the sun go down while you are still angry" (Ephesians 4:26).

Remember, anger chains you to the one with whom you are angry. Who wants to be chained to *that* person? If you're clinging to anger, release your grip and drop it into the Throw Away box.

Who Feels Better?

There was a knock on Georgia's door. It was Mary, a woman from church. Mary had a determined look on her face as she asked if Georgia had a minute to speak with her. "Sure. Do you want to come in?"

"No, this won't take long."

Those words were the introduction to an unexpected tirade. Mary explained she had been seeing a counselor to deal with some of the "issues" in her life. According to Mary, the counselor had listened intently for weeks as she poured out her feelings of inadequacy, anger, and resentment. Then the counselor had given Mary an assignment, one he guaranteed would make her feel much better. She was to confront anyone and everyone with whom she was angry and tell them exactly what was on her mind. Tonight was Georgia's turn. After her brief explanation, Mary proceeded to aggressively unload her anger on Georgia. It was obvious she felt justified, as she shot off her verbal weapon.

Needless to say, the confrontation was not done in love. Mary had put her anger and resentment into the Give Away box. It would have been much healthier to throw it away or seek resolution with Georgia in love. While the confrontation may have helped Mary feel better, there's a good chance she will regret her actions at some point in the future.

60

I liken Mary to a person carrying around a large bag of garbage. The bag is full and heavy, and Mary is tired of carrying it, looking for the quickest, easiest way to dispose of the mess. She finds relief in dumping her garbage on Georgia. Now Georgia's got a mess to clean up. A mess that's not even hers!

Giving away your anger to someone else is not appropriate or healthy. If my analogy holds true, it can also be very messy! Does that mean a confrontation is never warranted? No. The key lies in your motivation and delivery. If the desire is to hurt someone who has hurt you (or you think has hurt you), or if it is done to force that person to apologize, the motivation is wrong. If, in the words of Dr. Archibald Hart, you have "surrendered your right to hurt the person who hurt you," it is possible to confront in love. Confronting in love can bring resolution, dissolve anger, and heal. Other motivations only create more anger and a bigger mess.

A SPECIAL TREE

Ken lived in a small two-story bungalow near a neighborhood church. The only shade for his home was a walnut tree that grew on the church property. It was a beautiful, sturdy tree that was probably over seventy years old. Ken appreciated the shade this tree provided in the summer months and the beauty of the leaves in the spring and fall. Eventually, someone decided the old walnut tree and its discarded walnuts were a lawsuit waiting to happen. What if someone tripped and sued the church? This train of thought spread rapidly and before long the church board decided to have the tree cut down.

Ken was angry. He was very angry. How could those people think it was best to destroy that beautiful tree? Rather than confront, Ken chose to see if some good could come from the circumstances. He approached the church leaders and asked if he could have a portion of the walnut tree trunk. His idea was to see if he could use this large, crude piece of wood to turn his anger into something beautiful. Ken split and chiseled the wood. He carved, and sanded, and shaped it into a splendid work of art, a magnificent harp capable of creating beautiful music. After it was complete, he began the challenging task of learning to play the instrument.

I had the pleasure of hearing him play one day. He explained to those in attendance that he had only begun to master playing with his right hand and his left hand "just wasn't ready yet." He sat with that exquisite instrument, fashioned from the zeal of his anger, and played Jesus Loves Me.

As a result of Ken placing his anger into the Throw Away box, he made room for the beauty of the harp and his song. Getting rid of anger can make way for more beautiful things in your life. Maybe even things you can give away.

SIBLING RIVALRY

"Now Abel kept flocks, and Cain worked the soil. In the course of time Cain brought some of the fruits of the soil as an offering to the Lord. And Abel also brought an offering—fat portions from some of the firstborn of his flock. The Lord looked with favor on Abel and his offering, but on Cain and his offering he did not look with favor. So Cain was very angry, and his face was downcast. Then the Lord said to Cain, "Why are you angry? Why is your face downcast? If you do what is right, will you not be accepted? But if you do not do what is right, sin is crouching at your door; it desires to have you, but you must rule over it" (Genesis 4:2-7).

God encouraged Cain to master the sin he was embracing. He wanted him to admit his wrong and do what was right - to throw away his anger. Unfortunately, Cain did not choose to accept God's admonition. Instead he gave his anger away, killing his brother Abel in a rage. Now Cain said to his brother Abel, "Let's go out to the field." While they were in the field, Cain attacked his brother Abel and killed him."[4] God encourages us, through his Word, to take the anger from our hearts and dispose of it appropriately. Unfortunately, Cain made a poor choice.

HELP WITH A HEAVY LOAD

Many of the items I had stuffed into the Throw Away box were heavy and had been difficult to move from my heart. I have known people who were not able to dispose of the heart clutter by themselves. The process was too difficult and they needed help.

In contrast to the counselor who encouraged Mary to confront anyone and everyone with her anger, there are professionals who adopt a more biblical view. Finding a Christian counselor, psychologist, or member of the clergy to help you in the dejunking, can be a very positive option. Many times another person can be a big help in identifying clutter for the Throw Away box.

Perhaps a friend, teacher, spouse, or other family member relative can also help you sort through the clutter. It is important to note that for a Christian nonprofessional to qualify as a confidant two requirements must be met. (1) The person must love you and (2) want you to succeed. Unfortunately not everyone in your sphere of friends and family will fulfill both criteria. Be discriminating in allowing people to examine the clutter in your heart, mind, and memory.

Speaking of being discriminating, I saw an interesting example of this on a community billboard. The town marquee had a message that read:

CLEAN-UP DAY

SATURDAY, SEPTEMBER 12

OUTSIDERS PICKING UP WILL BE ARRESTED

I envisioned a visitor from out of state picking up a piece of paper she had dropped and being arrested. Surely that was not what the sign was warning against. Upon inquiry, I learned that officials were worried that an "unauthorized scavenger" might come to pick up, say, a refrigerator, drop it on his or her foot, and sue the town. Wow! They were definitely covering all the bases.

In the case of your personal "Clean-Up Day," you just might need an outsider to facilitate the process. That outsider will not be arrested! Christian books written by learned, licensed counselors have also been a big help to me through the years. Yes, I said through the years. Pitching clutter into the Throw Away bag is a lifelong process.

Reflection

♥

Time to Clear the Heart Clutter

Anger, resentment, and bitterness are potent emotions. Relax and try to remember the last time you felt any of those negative feelings. Can you recall what provoked them? Let God's Holy Spirit show you a constructive way to redirect those emotions. Jot down His ideas.

"Wherefore comfort yourselves together, and edify one another" (1 Thessalonians 5:11).

Find help! The Bible says we are to encourage and edify one another. Connecting with a Christian counselor, suitable friend, or relative is vital for your healing and emotional health.

6
THE THROW AWAY RULE

Whew! After going through all that clutter I could not imagine being able to fit one more thing into the Throw Away box. Thank goodness it was the largest one. I think I used every square inch. Sometimes it's tempting go back and dig through the junk, but as my mother used to say: Once you throw it away, no digging in the trash! That is the Throw Away rule.

If you find yourself second-guessing about the things you have tossed and trying to retrieve a few of them, stop before it is too late! The false guilt, the forgiven sins, the hurts and disappointments, the arrogance, selfishness, and anger belong right where they are – in the Throw Away box. Do not take them out and allow them to clutter your heart again.

LESSONS FROM SPAGHETTI

The importance of the Throw Away rule was illustrated perfectly one evening as my family and I enjoyed a spaghetti dinner. The menu for the evening included spaghetti, garlic bread, and tossed salad. As I finished cooking and set the table, I went to the refrigerator to gather the salad dressing.

It came as no surprise to me that I had several half- empty bottles of each kind of dressing. Since I know salad dressing bottles cannot multiply without help, I had always taken full responsibility for the lack of organization and the abundance of identical partially used bottles on my refrigerator door.

Then one day I observed one of our sons coming from the pantry, opening a new bottle of dressing even though there were two of that same variety already in the fridge. Maybe he found a fresh bottle more appealing or he had maybe not looked judiciously (or at all!), to see if there was already one open in the refrigerator. Having seen my other sons and their dad overlook other things on occasion, I began to wonder if this practice was gender-related.

Let me illustrate my hypothesis:

"Mom, where is my football shirt?"

"It's in your second drawer on the left-hand side."

"I looked there. It's not in that drawer."

"I'm sure it is. I just put it there yesterday."

"Honestly, Mom, I looked. It's not in my second drawer on the left-hand side."

At that point I leave my easy chair and traipse upstairs finding the shirt to be exactly where I'd instructed my son to look. As I walk downstairs holding the shirt in question I tell him, "Here it is. It was in your second drawer on the left-hand side under the blue t-shirt."

His response? "You didn't tell me I'd have to look *under* something!" And with that declaration, he feels totally vindicated. As I said, it would seem that hunting for non-living things is NOT a male attribute.

But, I digress! Let me get back to the spaghetti dinner. Noting the plethora of bottles in the fridge, I decided to consolidate them. I poured all the red dressing into one bottle and was attempting to do the same with the light-colored dressing when I realized there was more of this kind than one bottle's worth. So I filled a bottle to the top and put the remaining dressing in a bowl. Next I threw all the empty bottles into the trash. I was feeling very good about the small step I had taken toward increased organization.

Our meal was delicious and when the family had finished eating, each took his plate and scraped the remaining contents into the trash while I removed the serving dishes from the table. As I did, I noted there was a substantial amount of light-colored dressing still in the bowl. No problem, I thought. I had simply misjudged the amount of dressing and would need two bottles for that variety rather than just one. I had thrown the second bottle in the trash, but could easily retrieve it.

Oh, wait a minute. The empty salad dressing bottles were no longer lying on top. They were now lying under globs of pasta and spaghetti sauce. They, no doubt, had little pieces of carrot sticking to their sides, cucumber seeds dotting their labels, and crumbs of garlic bread glued to the open lids. The thought of rummaging through the garbage was revolting. I contemplated reaching into the trash, but quickly reconsidered and decided it was not worth it. Mother's words came alive to me and I gained a new appreciation for her rule "No digging in the trash!"

Reflection
♥
Time to Clear the Heart Clutter

I hope that you have pitched a few things into your Throw Away box as you have been reading. Have you been tempted to fish around in the mess for any of them? If so, write about those temptations and what you did in each instance. My challenge for you is to resist the temptation to dig in your Throw Away box. Leave those things where they belong!

7

Choose to Give Away Experience

After I closed the Throw Away box and threw it into the dumpster, it was time to start digging in my heart, mind, and memory to see if I had anything inside of me I could give away. Did I have anything someone else would might want or need? I

As a poked through the clutter I discovered I had life experiences I could put into the Give Away box to share. I'd gained a certain degree of wisdom from walking with the Lord for many years. Perhaps that wisdom could be valuable to others.

I quickly realized that giving experience away was a very delicate issue. Even though the wisdom might be helpful, if it had not been requested, the chances were great it would not be well received. The key was to wait for the invitation. My patience was rewarded, one day, with such an invitation.

Sharing a Day, Sharing Our Lives

The woman had a powerful voice and an equally powerful testimony. I had known her for years and she was scheduled to sing in a concert near our home. Prior to her arrival she gave me a call. "Hi Kendra, this is LeeAnn. I'm going to be very close to your home in about a month. I have a concert scheduled and will be arriving a day early. I was wondering if you'd be free for lunch that day." "I'd love to have lunch with you! Thanks for thinking of me. We can work out the details later."

As the day for the visit approached we chose the restaurant, set the time, and anticipated the fun we were going to have together. And we weren't disappointed. Our lunch was spent talking, laughing, and thoroughly enjoying one another's company. LeeAnn, at least ten years my junior, had questions about stages and phases of life I'd already experienced. I spoke candidly and shared the God-given wisdom I had gleaned from those experiences. Our time together was delightful and as we parted I was excitedly looking forward to her concert the following evening.

The concert was incredible. My friend's voice seemed to be richer and her songs more inspiring than ever before. During the worship set, she took a short break from singing to speak to the audience. "I love being in your area. Through the years I have made many friends. Just yesterday I had the opportunity to have lunch with an older Christian woman."

Her remarks caught me off guard. We had had lunch yesterday. She must be confused. Perhaps the lunch she was referring to occurred earlier that week. Then it dawned on me, *I* was the "older Christian woman." It was startling, but accurate.

As Christian women we are called to invest our time and talents, our experiences, and wisdom in the training of younger women. That's just what I had the privilege of doing. LeeAnn had questions about relationships, about family, and about the husband and children she would one day have. I had dipped into the Give Away box and offered experience that would help her as she walked that path in the future.

"Then they can urge the younger women to love their husbands and children" (Titus 2:4).

EXPERIENCE TEACHES US TO RESPOND

Anne was the director of a high-powered group of women. She was a hard-working leader who did her job well and encouraged those around her to do the same. As a teenager she had been in the youth ministry my husband and I led. Through the years she and I had maintained a relationship. It was not unusual for her to call and ask my advice on certain issues.

One afternoon, I received a call from her regarding a work situation. "I am really frustrated with one of my top performers. Marla took it upon herself to consolidate two assignments she was working on and to alter the projected date of completion. I haven't said a word to her yet but I'm questioning her judgment in the issue. Have you got time to hear some of the details and help me sort things out?" I did have time and she spent the next few minutes educating me on the finer points of the project. She didn't expect me to be an expert on industry-related subjects. She was simply looking for any wisdom I might have on dealing with Marla in a Christ-like manner.

"You've told me one of your goals is to avoid micromanaging those who report to you. You'll have to evaluate whether or not it was appropriate for Marla to consolidate the projects. It's important how you respond to her. You already made a good first decision by choosing not to react immediately. I think it might be helpful for you to ask the question 'What is my goal?' In this situation, it would seem your goal is to honestly evaluate the changes and see if they are reasonable. Discuss your views with Marla in an encouraging and positive way. Your goal is to represent Christ well. It is not to take

72

charge, embarrass Marla, or demand she do nothing without first checking with you."

Now, where did *I* learn that lesson? From experience! Where did I gain that experience? From failing to ask and answer the question What is my goal?

MOTHER TO MOTHER

A young mother approached a well-seasoned mother of six to ask her for a little advice. "You're such a great mom. All six of your kids are upstanding citizens. They are all walking with the Lord. They are all leaders in their churches and communities. I have a question for you. How did you become such a great mother?"

"That, my dear, is an easy question to answer. Two words—good choices."

The new mom seemed a little baffled and was not satisfied with the answer she had received. "But how did you make those good choices?"

"The answer is very simple. One word—experience."

Still not completely content with the answer, the inexperienced mom tried one more time. "And where did you get all that experience?"

"Bad choices!"

Many times we gain wisdom and experience from what I like to call Life Lessons- things we learn from our mistakes. With God's help they can be the source of experience leading to good choices. Experience, even if gained from bad choices, can be placed into the Give Away box to share with others.

A Hair-Raising Experience

It was Wednesday night and the high school Bible study was meeting in our home. Approximately twenty teenagers from several different churches were gathered for an hour of Bible study with treats to follow. As we were wrapping up, I jotted down the prayer concerns that were shared. A young man named Bob asked for prayer for the school play that was to be preformed in two weeks. I found his concern very interesting in light of what I had learned earlier that day.

Bob had a major part in the play. When he tried out months before, the director asked Bob if he would consider cutting his hair before the performance. It wasn't incredibly long, but the part as a law enforcement officer called for a clean-cut look. Bob told the director that cutting his hair would be no problem and he got the part. Now, weeks later, the director told him the time had arrived for a haircut. Bob balked at the idea. In fact, he told her he would not get a haircut. Reluctantly, the director gave Bob's part to another actor, relieving him of his responsibility. No one was happy about the situation including the substitute who didn't really want to perform. That poor guy had an extremely short amount of time to learn the lines and prepare for opening night.

After all the prayer requests had been shared and we had prayed, it was time for treats and conversation. Bob joined me in the kitchen and asked if I had heard the news about the change in the cast. I told him I had and he went on to offer his take on the unsettling issue. "I don't think it's fair to make me cut my hair. There's nothing wrong with the length of my hair. What do you think?"
"I don't think this has much to do with the length of your hair. I think it's a question of integrity."

"Integrity? What do you mean by that?"

74

"Well, I understand you and the director made an agreement during tryouts for the play. You agreed that when it came time for the performances you would get a haircut – one the director deemed appropriate. So, if you're refusing to get that haircut you're going back on your word. It isn't a question of whether or not it's fair for your director to demand a haircut. It's a question of whether or not you will keep your word. It's all about your integrity and it has been my *experience* that a person's integrity is more important than hair."

This gave Bob something to ponder. After a few minutes, he left the kitchen and joined some kids in the family room. A short while later, he returned. "Guess what I just did. I telephoned my mom and asked her to schedule me for a haircut tomorrow."

"Great choice! You need to remember, however, that you might not get your part in the play again. After all, you refused to get a haircut when the director first asked. Who knows what will happen? The important thing is that you're making the right choice."

Bob got a haircut the next day. The director reconsidered, gave him his part once back and the flustered replacement who had been desperately attempting to learn the lines, breathed a sigh of relief. The experience I'd pulled from my Give Away box was now part of Bob's to share with someone else some day.

DON'T FORCE IT

What if I had tried to force Bob to listen? What if I had chosen to share my experience without being asked? It is possible my unwanted, unsolicited advice would have fallen on deaf ears. When experience is requested we can take it from the Give Away box anticipating it will be appreciated.

75

Items placed in the Give Away box should not be forced upon some-one. It is better to let folks ask you or at least suggest some interest in what you have to share. Force-feeding others just pushes them away, possibly closing the door to sharing your experience in the future. Don't force feed people with your experience.

EXCUSE ME, DID I INTERRUPT?

As a storyteller by heart and profession I am often enamored with an experience and feel compelled to share it even when no request has been made. Years ago, I learned that if you are interrupted in the mid-dle of a story, you should wait until someone asks you to finish. That interruption might have occurred because no one wanted to hear the story in the first place.

Did I just say I "learned" that an interruption might indicate a lack of interest? I may have chosen the wrong verb. I have heard the word "learn" defined as a "a change in behavior." Perhaps I should have said, "Years ago, I was introduced to the concept that..." This change in wording would be more accurate because I did not immediately implement a change in my behavior even though I had heard what needed to change.

As is often the case, I soon had an opportunity to test the premise that had been presented. Before long I would try out the idea of wait-ing until someone requested that I finish a story I had begun.
I had been interrupted in the middle of recounting what I considered to be a very amusing experience. I waited patiently for someone to ask me to finish my delightful story. When that didn't happen, I had to exercise superhuman strength not to finish it anyway. The incident momentarily hurt my feelings because I was so sure I was giving away a great experience. The good news is that the next time it happened, I recovered sooner. My behavior was changing. It seemed as though I *was* actually learning. Giving away experience no one wants or needs

is not constructive. Instead wait for the right time, the right person, and the invitation to share.

A Life-Changing Experience

Consider the story in the Gospel of John of the man who was born blind. He was asked to share his experience. "They still did not believe that he had been blind and had received his sight until they sent for the man's parents. 'Is this your son?' they asked. 'Is this the one you say was born blind? How is it that now he can see?'"

"'We know he is our son,' the parents answered, 'and we know he was born blind. But how he can see now, or who opened his eyes, we don't know. Ask him. He is of age; he will speak for himself.'"

"A second time they summoned the man who had been blind. 'Give glory to God by telling the truth,' they said. 'We know this man is a sinner.'"

"He replied, 'Whether he is a sinner or not, I don't know. One thing I do know. I was blind but now I see!' (John 9:18-21,24-25).

Whether or not the men asking the questions came with pure motives, the blind man's response was so short and so direct there could be no interruption. The blind man was asked and gave away his experience —his life-changing, revolutionary encounter with Jesus.

REFLECTION
♥
TIME TO CLEAR THE HEART CLUTTER

Think of a positive experience from which you gained wisdom. Record the experience and what you learned. Then do the same with a negative experience where you learned a lesson from making a bad choice.

The blind man's response was so short and so direct there could be no interruption. Could you share your salvation story, your life-changing, revolutionary encounter with Jesus in a succinct manner that is easy to understand? Take some time to write your story here.

Be alert to the possibility that the Lord might want you to share that particular experience (your story) and perhaps others with people whose lives intersect yours.

8

CHOOSE TO GIVE AWAY MEMORIES

As I sifted through the clutter in my heart, mind, and memory I discovered something else that could be placed into the Give Away box. I had memories stored away. Memories can be positive or negative. Some deserve no better destiny than the Throw Away box while others are treasures to be shared. I found several of those treasures and put them into the Give Away box.

TELL ME THE STORY OF WHEN...

In 1990 something happened to our family that had never happened before. My husband flew a tanker for the United States Air Force Reserves, a plane that refuels military jets. In August of that year, the country of Iraq invaded Kuwait. Prior to that day I had never heard of Kuwait and consequently had never imagined this country could have an impact on our lives in central Illinois. As the history books tell us, Kuwait was overrun and many United States forces were called into action. Within days of the invasion, John was headed to the Middle East. Our boys were all in grade school and the idea of their dad being gone to a potential war zone was not only novel but also frightening. Each of them had a different reaction to their dad's absence.

I distinctly remember when our oldest son asked me to share a memory with him, a memory that actually belonged to his dad. It was the story of his infamous riding wound.

"Mom, could you please tell me the story of when Dad was little and was riding his horse, Trigger, and Trigger ran Dad into the barbed wire fence and how Dad got his leg caught on the fence and ripped a big hole in his thigh and how he still has a scar there today? Could you please tell that story Mom?"

You might find it interesting to note that the memory he requested was precisely the one he had just recounted. There were no more facts or details. That was it!

It was the story of Dad's famous riding wound. Our son already knew the story. What was he actually asking me to do? Maybe this was what he was saying. "Mom, I miss Dad. If you tell me a story he has told me many times before, if you'll share that memory with me, maybe I won't miss him so much."

I heard the words he spoke and I sensed what he was actually saying so I told his Dad's memory. I repeated almost word for word what I had just heard. And our son felt better.

Memories are wonderful things to share. That evening I discovered the comforting power of memories given away and our son's response was one I'll always remember. We went on to create a new memory together to put into our Give Away boxes.

When I finished the story of Dad and Trigger, we sat quietly for just a minute or two before he broke the silence. "Mom, you don't have a whole lot of great memories from when you were a kid, do you?" He had come to that conclusion knowing I had been raised in the home of a functional alcoholic. He surmised that the majority of my childhood memories were not positive. To my surprise, I became a bit defensive in reaction to his question. "Oh, I have some pretty good ones."

"Well, I'm just glad that when I'm a grown-up and my kids ask me about when I was a kid I'll have lots of good memories to tell."

Was I blessed by that reflection from our young son? You better believe it! I'm grateful I have that memory to share.

THE FAT FAIRY

Among the good memories of growing up were the traditional visits from the Fat Fairy. She was a combination of Santa Claus, the Tooth Fairy, the Easter Bunny, and every other delightful mythical character. She did not take herself too seriously, as evidenced by her unflattering name, but she did supply money for missing teeth, poems during Advent, and at least one wrapped gift under the Christmas tree. Who was she? She was my Mom. Can you guess who the Fat Fairy was when our kids were growing up? Yes, it was me! Today, it is still me but, now they know the Fat Fairy is really Grandma KK.

DOUGHNUTS, DOUGHNUTS, DOUGHNUTS

You can choose to create a memory for your family. We did just that during the Christmas season. One particular tradition began when our two older sons were just five and three years old. We decided to give homemade doughnuts to friends and family as Christmas gifts.

The first year or two were experiments in family cooking. I decided we should make a recipe I found in my *Better Homes & Gardens* cookbook, multiplying the serving size by ten! The time and space required to accomplish this were two things I failed to calculate. I also had no clue that this exciting adventure the boys were eagerly anticipating would become boring so quickly. As the doughnuts took shape, thanks to the diligent work of Dad the Doughnut Cutter, we ran into a dilemma. Where do you put all the little masterpieces while they rise?

The dining room table was our first and most logical solution. We soon discovered it held approximately ten dozen doughnuts. The problem was we were making twenty dozen! The dining room floor seemed to be our only other option. We spread out sheets of waxed paper over the hardwood and I wondered how the doughnuts would ever rise on our drafty floor. And what would we do if someone surprised us with a morning visit? Our home was a modest bungalow. The doughnuts filled the dining room table and the wax paper covered floor in the dining room, portions of the living room, and down the hallway. To the untrained eye it would appear that doughnuts had taken over our home and were holding us hostage.

In spite of the challenge we successfully finished the task at hand. The doughnuts rose, we fried them, frosted them, and filled eight very large trays. Then everyone in the family chose two households to receive our culinary gift. We wrapped the trays in cellophane, tied each one with a ribbon and we set off to make our deliveries.

The first year wasn't an easy one, but it definitely wasn't the most challenging. Imagine the scene I just described to you – wall to wall doughnuts rising at their leisure – plus a crawling baby. The additional challenge didn't dissuade us. Our little crawler soon learned how to navigate around the edible gifts and our doughnut-making memory continued. After seven years of making the adventure work in our little home, we moved to a home with a much larger kitchen and dining room, and the process evolved. We increased the number of doughnuts to fourteen times the recipe. As the number grew, so did the boys. I don't know that they stay enthralled for any longer periods of time than they did in their preschool days, but the fact we no longer had to deal with a toddler made things easier. Making those doughnuts year after year became a memory they will have forever – perfect for the Give Away box.

I will be the first to admit, not every memory we created for our family was picture perfect. We were imperfect parents. We continue to take the opportunity to apologize to our kids as we realize mistakes that were made. The truth is we are all the product of imperfect parents. That means you probably have a memory or two that is less than perfect. With the Lord's help and, if needed, the help of a qualified Christian counselor, those unpleasant memories can be healed and forgiveness can be extended. If you discover one of those less- than-perfect memories as you search through your heart clutter, pray that God help you through it. Perhaps, someday you will be able to put it into the Give Away box as an experience that can help someone else.

Memories Are Made of This

Our family photo albums are a combination of pictures and journaling. To celebrate each son's high school graduation, I gave him an album, recording his growth, and achievements, his family, and friends. Those albums house a rich heritage and function to keep memories alive.

The boys also received a special gift from their uncle. Among his many talents, John's younger brother has the ability to produce masterpieces on video. He created a video story for each of the boys using still photographs, portions of home movies, and footage taken by the school's videographers. He dubbed in a great soundtrack that played in the background of the interviews he had conducted. The videos are precious classics.

I laughed as I watched their family and friends retell stories of their escapades. There were classroom adventures, sports sagas, and the celebration of longtime friendships. Each video contained advice for success in the future—some legitimate, some given totally for comic relief. My laughter turned to tears of gratefulness when John recounted memories of praying for each of our sons even before they were born, praying each would accept Jesus Christ as his Savior.

Memories are a wonderful gift to put into the Give Away box and share with others.

WALL OF MEMORIES

Walking up the stairs in our home, I am greeted by walls of memories. On the west, south, and the east are large frames filled with a collage of family pictures. When our oldest son was born I gave John the first one for Christmas. The gift was so well received I repeated it every year until our youngest son graduated from high school and went to college. Those frames record memories of the boys' athletic adventures, musical performances, and assorted pets. There are pictures of family vacations, of special friends, and of extended family who have touched our lives through the years. There are pictures, for example, of our eight-day Canadian wilderness canoe trip. That was the trip we took instead of buying carpeting. I'm a little ashamed I even had the debate with myself—carpet versus Canada. Thank goodness Canada and its memories won the contest.

Memories, so many of them, right there on the wall. The frames line the hallway of the open staircase, hung in chronological order of our family history. On more than one occasion I have spotted John standing and studying this pictorial history. How quickly those years have passed! Our family now consists of three grown men, three daughters-in-law, and nine grandchildren and counting.

Staking Their Claim

It is important to remember the things God has done in your life. They are precious memories. When I was in high school youth ministry, I wanted to help those teenagers keep the memory of God-incidences alive. Some had come to a saving knowledge of Christ at a youth event or meeting. Many had witnessed a verse from God's word come alive, a verse that was beneficial in their walk with Jesus. I wanted them to remember those are heart-changing experiences. That is why I encouraged them to "drive a stake behind the barn."

Perhaps you are confused by my instruction. Let me explain. In our rural community, it could have literally meant hammering a stake behind one of the out buildings on a student's family farm. For the teenagers who lived in town, it could have meant pounding a stake into the ground behind the garage. And my directive did not have to be literal. The idea was simply to encourage the kids to create a concrete and personal reminder of the reality of their experience with God, an Ebenezer.

After the Lord intervened in a battle with the Philistines, the Bible records the action taken by Samuel. 1 Samuel 7:12 – "Then Samuel took a stone and set it up between Mizpah and Shen, and called its name Ebenezer, saying, 'Thus far the Lord has helped us.'"

Satan wants to steal the very real moments you have had with God. He enjoys convincing you that the Lord's ability to divinely intervene in your life is merely wishful thinking or a figment of your imagination that can never come to pass. Combat his lies by recording your heart change. It can take the form of a "stake behind the barn" or a page in your journal. And take every opportunity presented to share your

God moments with others, so that your memory has the chance to become their blessing too.

SHARING THE JOY OF YOUR SALVATION

If you declare with your mouth, "Jesus is Lord," and believe in your heart that God raised him from the dead, you will be saved" (Romans 10:9).

Confessing your faith helps confirm the reality of your salvation. It helps keep it alive in your memory. "Restore to me the joy of your salvation and grant me a willing spirit, to sustain me" (Psalms 51:12). If you feel as though you have lost the joy of your salvation, the joy of receiving God's gift of eternal life, recapture it by reading the account in your journal or glancing at the stake behind the barn.

"He has caused his wonders to be remembered; the Lord is gracious and compassionate" (Psalms 111:4).

Your memory of that real encounter with God is a treasure. It is a memory that belongs in the Give Away box, ready to share with others. The stake, literal or figurative, is there to see and touch just like the stone set up by Samuel. In a sense it is guarding the memory, protecting it from being stolen.

"Remember the wonders he has done, his miracles, and the judgments he pronounced" (Psalm 105:5).

REFLECTION
♥
TIME TO CLEAR THE HEART CLUTTER

Take time to record one of your favorite childhood memories. Why does that memory bring you joy? Could that memory bring someone else comfort and joy? If the answer is yes, ask God to provide an opportunity for you to share it.

God's word is "alive and active" (Hebrews 4:12). When has it spoken directly to you? What was the personal message and how did it change your attitude or direction? Use the space below to "drive a stake behind the barn." When God opens the door, share the memory and how it changed your life.

Who might benefit from hearing the memory you have of the Word of God coming alive? Make a list of people who came to mind. Now pray for a God-supplied opportunity to share your memory with someone. Ask the Lord to help you recognize the opportunity when it comes.

9

CHOOSE TO GIVE AWAY ENCOURAGEMENT

During those summers of cleaning my room, I often thought that if I had completed at least half of the job, it was better than having not done anything at all. My flawed reasoning led me to believe that I really didn't *need* to finish the de-junking process since what I had done seemed a significant enough improvement. As you can imagine, that logic got me nowhere.

While applying the process of cleaning out the clutter in my heart, mind, and memory, I realized this task was susceptible to the same false premise. I felt certain I had done enough sorting and sifting, but God's spirit prompted me to continue. So, I searched for more to give away and, in doing so, discovered encouragement.

ENCOURAGED TO BE ENCOURAGERS

One of Paul's first letters to the Thessalonians instructed them to "encourage one another and build each other up.."[5] He did not say, "discourage one another and tear each other down" as I have witnessed on occasion, even in the family of God. In a different letter, Paul warns the church of Ephesus, "Do not let any unwholesome talk come out of your mouths, but only what is helpful for building others up according to their needs, that it may benefit those who listen"[6] (Ephesians 4:29). The world does enough discouraging and it doesn't need the help of believers.

There are endless examples of how to promote positivity in our personal surroundings. The workplace is known all too well for its negative environment. When was the last time you or a co-worker or was applauded at work for a job well done? How frequently do you experience or witness senseless conflicts with colleagues or management? Too often the workplace is permeated with a negative atmosphere instead of a positive one.

When was the last time your child came home from school elated over some encouragement he or she had received? When was the last time that same child came home discouraged and deflated? My guess is the latter has happened too often.

When we started a family I chose to be an at-home mom, but there were times when I was discouraged by my decision. In fact, I can still remember my husband announcing his discovery of why being a homemaker was so tough. He explained that a significant portion of my "job" in the home was to see that everything ran smoothly. Consequently, no one noticed. But, let me get behind with the wash or let the meals become boring and repetitive and someone was quick to note it *and* voice their displeasure.

"Peanut butter and jelly again?"

"Where is my baseball uniform? I thought you said you were going to wash it?"

"Golly, Mom, what in the world have you been doing?"

My husband's conclusion was simple yet profound: "Being a home-maker is tough because we only notice when you're not doing it perfectly." As discouraging as this fact is, it's a part of life. Living here on earth we will encounter many discouragements. Life isn't always fair! But, we can find peace in knowing that God knows our struggles.

There are situations you encounter that tear you down, but it's important to remember you are called to "encourage one another and build each other up." It can take a great deal of encouragement to overcome a little slice of discouragement. That makes the call to be an encourager even more important. You have it inside of you. I know you do. It's time to put encouragement into the Give Away box. You'll be encouraged as you encourage others!

The Power of Encouragement

Years ago at a baseball game I saw an amazing example of the power of encouragement. John was the coach and the athletes were between twelve and thirteen years old. The league rules stipulated that if your team did not have enough players and the opponents had more than enough, you could borrow a player for the game. This system obviously had strengths as well as weaknesses. It did make the teams equal in number and it gave a potential bench-sitter on the overpopulated team an opportunity to start and play the entire game. The problem was that it pulled at the loyalty of the temporarily traded ballplayer.

John's team found itself one player short for the first game of a tournament. John went to the opposing bench where three boys were "riding the pines." "Would one of you guys like to play for us tonight?" Two of the boys immediately said no, leaving the third, Donald, to respond. Deep in the recesses of his thirteen-year-old heart, I'm sure he was feeling the potential satisfaction of getting an entire game of playing time, in contrast to the one inning he was destined for on his own team. At the same time, he realized he would be a traitor if, miraculously, he performed well for the opponent. After evaluating the pros and cons, Donald joined John's team and was put at the end of the batting order.

By the second inning Donald was up to bat facing his own team's number one pitcher. As he approached home plate John, an encourager by nature, began to cheer. "You can do it, Donald! You can get a hit. Stand right in there. You can do it!"

Miraculously, Donald did do it! He slammed one into the outfield and shot off to first base. Although I'd not witnessed any of his previous "at bats," my guess is that none of his other hits were as impressive or brought such accolades. Under John's skillful direction and encouragement, Donald stole second, his adopted team cheering him on. The next batter got a hit and Donald took off for third as John urged him toward the base: "Slide, Donald, slide!"

The third baseman tried to tag Donald, but he slid under the ball, safe at third base. As he stood up and dusted himself off, he was smiling from ear to ear. The roar of his temporary teammates, the encouraging applause of his short-term coach, and the cheering crowd added to his pleasure and pride. "I knew you could do it, Donald!" The next batter's hit sent Donald on his way to home plate where he scored a run. When he returned to the bench, John congratulated him. "You know, Coach. I've been working this summer and I think I got that good hit because my wrists are stronger." "I'll bet you're right," was John's affirming and encouraging reply.

Donald, destined to warm the bench for his own team, had temporarily switched loyalties and scored a run. Could he have done it without the encouragement? We will never know. Personally, I don't think he would have made it to first base.

THE GUTTER THEORY

Encouragement is really a very simple thing. Sometimes just having someone believe you can do it (whatever "it" is) can be enough to convince you too. Unfortunately it would seem there are people unwilling or unable to be encouraging. I have discovered a common denominator among the discouragers. They are discouraged themselves. These people spend a great deal of time and energy putting others down in the hope they will feel better in the process.

Discouragers are perfect illustrations of the "The Gutter Theory", a theory that states people who are in the gutter do everything they can to pull others down with them. These folks need encouragement as much as or maybe even more than everyone else. Maybe they don't feel deserving of encouragement. Either way, their behavior is a prime example that no one wants to be in the gutter alone. Misery really does love company!

For years my refrigerator door sported one of my favorite cartoons. In frame one we see a little boy, who is obviously discouraged, standing by his mom. Mom realizes something needs to be done so she asks, "What's wrong?"

In frame two the young man answers his mother's question. "No one likes me."

Frame three: "That's not true. I like you!"

Final frame: "Of course you do. That's your job!!"

92

As cute as this cartoon is, and as much as I enjoy encouraging my children, encouragement is not just the job of moms. Encouragement is the job and privilege for all Christians. We aren't called to "like" everyone the way we like our children, but we are called to be encouragers. Encouragement belongs in the Give Away box. And unlike the sharing of experience, you don't need to wait until it's requested. Encouragement can be freely given.

STEP-BY-STEP ENCOURAGEMENT

Have you ever had the pleasure of watching a child take his first steps? It is always obvious that the big moment is close at hand. I remember when our youngest began to walk. John and I had alerted his older brothers that it wouldn't be long and they were on the lookout for those first steps.

One Sunday after church I went into the kitchen to prepare dinner while John settled in front of the television to catch the football game. The boys grabbed their Matchbox cars and joined their dad in the living room for a little "road racing" before lunch. Within minutes, the youngest had abandoned his cars and crawled over to the couch. As he pulled himself up, he glanced around the room as though taking roll. No words were spoken, but I imagine he was thinking something like, "Mom, you're going to need to get out of the kitchen to see this. Dad, look over here. Hey brothers, are you watching?"

His silent roll call somehow managed to get everyone's attention. Once all eyes were on him, he turned and steadied himself. Letting go of the couch, he took one step… and down he went. The crowd went wild!!!

"Great job! Give me five, big guy!"

"That was super!"

"Hooray, he took a step!"

Without missing a beat, he crawled back over to the couch, pulled himself up, and glanced around the room to be sure every eye was on him. Then he turned once again, steadied himself, and took one step. Then another step and down he went. This accomplishment was almost too much for his adoring fans. He was a super-star!

"Yay! You're the best!"

"That was great walking!"

"Two steps this time! You went twice as far!"

That accomplishment occurred many years ago and walking was only the beginning. This feat was soon followed by running, hopping, skipping, and dancing (an important achievement I have appreciated at more than one wedding). How was he able to master all those skills and more? He kept trying and we kept applauding and encouraging.

I have wondered what would have happened if, instead, the scene had gone something like this…The wordless roll call captured everyone's attention. With all eyes on him, the he turned, steadied himself, let go of the couch, took a step, and sat down hard. He waited expectantly for the response of the crowd.

"What were you trying to do, walk?"

"Yea, was that supposed to be walking?"

"Please don't try again. You might hurt yourself."

Quite confused and a little dismayed, the youngster crawled back to the couch, pulled himself up, and glanced around the room. Once again, he turned, steadied himself, and took one step. Then another step…and down he went.

"Please do not do that again. You obviously can't walk. I think maybe you're too short."

"Thank goodness he is short. He keeps falling down."

"That will be enough of your silliness. You cannot walk so just quit trying."

What discouragement! Does that second scene make you angry, or frustrated, or genuinely disgusted with every one but the poor little guy who is trying to learn to walk? Of course it does! Thankfully, very few people would ever speak to a one-year-old that way.

Still, there are folks who choose to speak just as disparagingly to others without a second thought.

"*You*'re going to bake a cake for the church bazaar? Why don't you get one from the Bakery? I really don't think your cake will bring much money for the mission outreach!"

"Why did you make a B- in spelling? That is ridiculous. Spelling is just memorization."

Discouragement is offered rather than encouragement. Remember! "Therefore encourage one another and build each other up…" even in your own home. Perhaps it should be *especially* in your own home.

THE PERFECT NAME

More than once in the Bible we are introduced to someone who was first called by one name and then by another. Joseph, a Levite from Cyprus, is one example. The apostles called him Barnabas, which means "son of encouragement." Barnabas "sold a field he owned and brought the money and put it at the apostles' feet."[7] His selflessness and offering was an encouragement to those who traveled preaching the word of God and building up the church. "News of this reached the church in Jerusalem, and they sent Barnabas to Antioch. When he arrived and saw what the grace of God had done, he was glad and encouraged them all to remain true to the Lord with all their hearts" (Acts 11:22-23).

REFLECTION
❤
TIME TO CLEAR THE HEART CLUTTER

Think back to the time when someone gave you the encouragement you needed. Record the circumstance, the encouragement, and the result of the encouragement. Now write a note of thanks to that encourager.

Look for an opportunity to give away encouragement today. It could be a Facebook message or post, a text, an email, a phone call, a lunch date, or a handwritten note. The next time you open this book record the incident, how you felt being an encourager, and if possible, the reaction of the one receiving the encouragement.

♥

10

Choose to Give Away Your Faith

When I was sorting and sifting through the various things in my heart, mind, and memory I realized that faith would be a perfect addition to the Give Away box. What made me so certain adding faith was a good idea? Because I had the privilege and blessing of being the recipient as someone chose to share faith, to put it into the Give Away box.

A Summertime Meeting

As a young girl I was taught the value and satisfaction of hard work. Growing up in central Illinois provided me with a job opportunity when I was only thirteen years old. At that age I could be employed by one of the seed corn companies to detassel corn. Many of you are probably scratching your heads in wonderment; so let me explain what the job entails.

Hybrid seed corn companies want to control the pollination of corn plants by preventing them from self-pollination – the process of pollen traveling from the top of the plant (the tassel) down the silk to the ear. Many hybrid seed companies hire teenagers to ride on funny-looking machines or walk through the rows of corn to and remove the tassels, hence, de-tasseling.

The job is hard work. The starting time each day is ridiculously early, and the conditions (wet, sharp corn leaves in the early morning hours followed by sweltering heat at midday) are undesirable. But this job has at least one redeeming feature. Detasselers are paid well. Add to this the fact that, typically, no other job is available when you're only thirteen, fourteen, and fifteen and it begins to look pretty good. When you reach sixteen, however, several doors open for employment. You could, for example, take senior lifesaving and become a lifeguard at the local swimming pool.

The summer I was sixteen I carefully weighed the pros and cons of each job. I already had extensive knowledge about detasseling because I had done that since I was thirteen. The pool job had some definite plusses. The hours were good with a starting time late enough to encourage any teenager to become nocturnal. The conditions were practically perfect with plenty of sunshine and socialization. OK, the pay was poor, but after weighing both options for at least 10 seconds, I signed up for senior lifesaving.

The course was three weeks long. We learned Red Cross life-saving skills, were instructed in first aid, and worked to increase our swimming stamina. The last three days constituted the final exam. We had a written test, an endurance swim, and finally on the last day, we were scheduled to "rescue the victim."

When we arrived at the pool on the final day I noticed our instructor was not alone. Standing next to him was a very good- looking young man with blond hair and big muscles. Our instructor introduced him as his younger brother who was there to help with the test. As I moved toward the younger brother's line, I noticed I was not alone. It seemed that every other girl had the same idea. So I got into his line first, and, as I like to say at our house, "Mom got Dad in a cross-chest carry and never let go."

That's how I met my husband. We had our first date that afternoon and were married four years later. Most of the dating years were good ones, but I do remember one incident that left me a little uncertain about the possible future of our relationship.

I was a senior in high school and dealing with a major catastrophe. It has been my experience that most of the major catastrophes teenage girls go through will soon be forgotten. I considered my disaster serious enough to share it with John, my boyfriend at the time. Although I too have forgotten the actual crisis, I vividly remember his response. He listened intently to my situation, drew in a deep breath, and suggested I pray about it.

The idea was very foreign to me as I was not a believer and the suggestion seemed rather ridiculous. I kept my thoughts to myself. "Pray about it? What does God have to do with this whole thing? Surely He is too busy with gravity and the galaxy to care about what's bothering me."

After John left my home that evening, I wondered what would become of our romance. Pray about it?! I had never heard of anything so silly.

Our romance did not disintegrate however, because I refocused my vision on what I believed to be his finer points (I already mentioned he was really cute, right?) I decided it was okay if he was a little bit different. And he was obviously unaware of the scripture warning believers to avoid being "unequally yoked" (2Corinthians 6:14).

THE BIG DIFFERENCE

What was different about him? He was a Christian. At sixteen he had accepted Christ as his Savior when an evangelist visited the little church his family attended. John talked with the Lord and did his best to listen to Him from that point forward, but he received very little instruction in God's word. My initial reaction to John's advice is exactly what Paul was warning the church of Corinth about when he told them, Do not be yoked together with unbelievers. For what do righteousness and wickedness have in common? Or what fellowship can light have with darkness?"[8]

Four years after we met, he yoked up with me. We were married and one week after our wedding we drove to west Texas so John could begin pilot training for the United States Air Force. Becoming an Air Force pilot was a thrilling, challenging adventure. He was having a wonderful time learning about jets and about the art of piloting such an impressive piece of hardware. He was also driving me crazy!

John had a peace about him that was more than I could understand. He absolutely refused to worry about the things I felt warranted a certain degree of concentrated worry. He seemed to pray about everything, even things like where we would live and where I could find a job. Worst of all, he exemplified the fruits of the Spirit described in Galatians 5 – love, joy, peace, patience, kindness, goodness, faithfulness, gentleness, and self-control – almost all the time.

One evening when we had only been married a few months I asked John to explain why he was so content and I was so completely miserable. It was just the opening he had been waiting for. "I think the difference might be that I have accepted Christ as my Savior and I'm not sure you have done that yet."

He didn't talk about denominations or their differences. He didn't tell me I was bound for hell and he extended some gentle kindness by saying he wasn't "sure I had done that yet." John simply lived his faith in front of me. I asked him to give me the reason for the hope and peace he had and he responded with gentleness and respect. My reply was simple, "Yes, that probably is the difference. What do we do now?" The answer was a simple prayer of repentance and faith. That's what we did next.

OPPORTUNITIES ABOUND

There are plenty of opportunities for you to put your faith into the Give Away box to share with others. Sometimes they are structured, planned, and calculated. Other times, they're spontaneous.

When our kids were little, we went to the library every week in the summer. It was a fun outing that we all looked forward to it. One sunny day as we laughed while building out our pile of books, the librarian came over to join us. "You always seem so filled with joy. What's your secret?"

Wow! What an opening. What a perfect opportunity to share about the love of Christ. I'm guessing you're probably thinking I took full advantage of the moment, but please don't be too disappointed. My sorry reply was simply, "Gee, I don't know. I guess I just got enough sleep last night."

Boy, that's really spiritual. A reply like that is bound to make a difference for the kingdom of God. Nope! I realized almost immediately I had missed an opportunity. Later in the week, I was reading 1 Peter 3:15 and was convicted as I thought back to my lost opportunity. "But in your hearts revere Christ as Lord. Always be prepared to give an answer to everyone who asks you to give the reason for the hope that you have. But do this with gentleness and respect." I had missed an opportunity. I wasn't prepared.

After reading that verse, I asked God to give me another opportunity to share my faith with the librarian. I had learned from past experience that if, in a sense, you miss the 8:05, God might send the 9:05.

Sure enough, on one of the next visits the librarian presented me with another opening. This time I was prepared. Faith is a good thing to put into the Give Away box.

Sharing your faith, putting into the Give Away box can result in a variety of responses from different people. I gladly embraced the faith my husband shared and the librarian welcomed my response. But that is not always the case.

AND THEN THERE WAS JOE

Joe had been a friend of our family for several years. He was a gruff older man who successfully hid his tender heart from almost everyone who knew him. For whatever reason, he couldn't hide it from me. He and his wife were very private but our paths intersected often enough that our family grew to know them and love them.

Joe and Beth were completely "unchurched." I don't believe they ever went to church, not even on Christmas or Easter. They knew we were regular attenders, but that didn't seem to matter to them one way or another. If they had been questioned, my guess is that they would have called us good friends even though the connection between this elderly couple and our family was not daily or even weekly.

When Joe and Beth needed help and we were aware of the situation, we did what we could. When Beth was struggling with health problems I was able to take her to the doctor on several occasions. In gratitude, Joe and Beth reciprocated by finding ways to be a blessing to our three sons.

After each visit together I would always leave them with a simple, "We love you," as a reminder that we cared. They never responded to my statement and I never expected them to. I'm sure they found the idea of our family loving them slightly unusual and probably a little uncomfortable too. I often told this elderly couple I loved them but I never told them how much Jesus loved them.

Then one night I had a dream. In my dream Joe and Beth were driving down the highway in their beat-up car and were in a fatal accident. The dream continued and both of them, though dead, began talking. "Why didn't you tell us? Why didn't you tell us about Jesus? We're dead and now it's too late!"

I woke from that dream with a start, replaying all the details in my mind. When morning came, I relayed the dream to John. "God spoke to me in that dream. I don't think Joe and Beth are on the verge of a fatal car accident. That's not what God was trying to tell me. He was letting me know I need to share my faith with them."

God had never spoken to me in a dream before but there was no doubt in my mind it was a message from Him. In spite of that, I was not very excited about the task of sharing my faith with Joe and Beth. Our relationship was comfortable. They both liked me and weren't threatened by my quiet faith. Maybe I was a little threatened by their lack of faith. So many questions flitted through my mind.

"What if I share my faith and they laugh at me?"

"What if they sever all ties with our family? The boys would miss their kindness."

"What if they get angry with me?"

"What if they belittle me?"

104

Those questions were not from God. They came from my self-centered attitude, my insecurity, my pride, and probably from the Enemy himself. Ultimately, I realized there was one more question I had to answer and it was by far the most important one. "Kendra, you say I come first in your life. You say you love Joe and Beth yet you fail to tell them about me. Which of those two statements is a lie?"

Which one *is* a lie? Humbled, I realized I could not leave Jesus out of the friendship any longer, so I began to look for an opening to give away my faith, an opportunity to share it with Joe and Beth. Within weeks of the dream, I volunteered to take Beth to a nearby community to do some shopping. The outing was long enough that we had plenty of time to talk. While we walked and talked, I told her my story of repentance and redemption. I told her of God's plan of salvation and also about my dream. She listened intently and thanked me for sharing these things with her. The conversation continued a few minutes longer and then the topic shifted. Seeds had been planted.

A few days later I noticed Joe's truck in the parking lot of a small local shop where he sometimes worked. He was the only one there and it was the opportunity I had been seeking. I told him of my dream and then proceeded to do a monologue on salvation. I closed by telling him about the challenge I believe God had given me weeks earlier. "You say I come first in your life. You say you love Joe and Beth yet you fail to tell them about me. Which of those two statements is a lie?"

Joe just stood there staring at me. He didn't seem to be angry or even more than politely interested. "I'm here today because I didn't want to be a liar. Do you understand what I've told you?"

His reply was short and to the point. "Yes, I do." That was it, and that was the end of the conversation.

I hugged him and left. The conversation didn't end as I had hoped and secretly planned. There was no sinner's prayer or repentant attitude. I'd carefully retrieved my faith from the Give Away box and had held it out to Joe. He took a look at it and left it right there in my hand. When this happens, as it sometimes will, don't let it dissuade you from giving away faith in the future. Our focus is to please the Lord and do His will so that we are the fragrance of Christ. It isn't your job to convince, debate, or coerce. Your responsibility is to live your faith, share it, and lead with grace without compromising the truth.

That is what I continue to do with Joe and Beth. It seems as though the conversations I had with them haven't changed their thinking or their lives - yet. But, they didn't break off the ties of friendship either. Now I can be assured they have heard the gospel message. Now they can choose how they will respond to it. When we put our faith into the Give Away box, we don't always know when or if another will take it out.

"I planted the seed, Apollos watered it, but God has been making it grow" (1 Corinthians 3:6).

TIMING IS EVERYTHING

On another occasion I put my faith into the Give Away box in the form of a letter written to someone important in my life. A week or so later when I saw my friend, I received a rather condescending reply to the words I'd written. "That's nice, Kendra. I'm glad this religion stuff works for you. I'm guessing someday you'll outgrow it."

I don't have to tell you this person was older than me. As I listened to his words it was as though he was patting me on the head, patronizing me. He obviously wanted no part of this "religion stuff" I

106

was sharing. I had told him of my faith in that letter and years later I was to discover that he'd kept it in his dresser drawer. While he didn't immediately accept the truth I was offering, he didn't completely wash his hands of it either. My faith rested in the Give Away box waiting for him to respond to God's love.

Eight years after he received my letter a crisis arose in his life. He was extremely ill – so sick the doctors gave him no chance of recovery. On one of my many visits to his bedside I found the perfect opportunity to replay the contents of my letter and present the gospel once again. This time, his response was quite different. Instead of demeaning my faith, he embraced it and prayed to receive Jesus as his Savior. Days later, his time on this earth came to an end. When you put your faith into the Give Away box you never know when it might be received.

As tough as it is for us adults and "seasoned" believers to share our faith, imagine how bold you must be to have the courage to extend your faith as a young person. A teenage boy I know did just that. He took the opportunity to share about Christ with a teammate of his after football practice one day. The response was less than enthusiastic. "I know you're probably right about this Jesus stuff but I'm just not ready for it yet."

When would he be ready? Would he someday find himself face to face with a deadly disease and then decide he was ready? That wasn't the case for this young man. The reluctant football player's life was abruptly taken in an automobile accident. The friend who had shared his faith was devastated. "Why didn't he choose Jesus before it was too late?"

In an effort to comfort my young friend, I realized once again you can never know when someone might receive the faith you have shared the faith, the faith you've put into the Give Away box. "We won't know what transpired during your friend's last seconds of life. It's possible that in that brief time between recognizing the impending accident and the impact itself, your friend might have spoken the name of Jesus in faith, believing He was and is the Son of God and his Savior." In truth, we don't know what happened. We don't know if in the last second of his life this teenage boy reached into the Give Away box and snatched out faith in God as his own. We do know there was faith in that box. His friend and teammate had put it in for him to grasp. Giving away your faith can make an eternal difference you might never realize while you are on earth. Don't hesitate to share yours!

No Assumption

It is a great blessing to be invited to speak to others about the love and grace of God. Regardless of the setting, I try not to overlook an opportunity to give away my faith, to share it with the audience, large or small. It is a mistake to assume everyone has made a profession of faith. I learned that through experience, an experience when my initial assumption had not been correct.

A young man volunteered to bring an inspiring message to his church. He asked if I would have time to read it and give him some helpful hints. We met together and he read his message to me. It was very sterile and quite boring; it needed more meat and meaning. I racked my brain deciding how I could communicate that to him, help him improve, and not crush his desire to speak.

"I had an idea while you were reading your message. It would be a different slant than what you've taken, but I think it might be meaningful. What if you simply told the congregation about your experience, about when you accepted Christ as your Savior? Testimonies of faith can be very powerful."

He looked at me with pleading eyes. That was when I realized the possibility existed he had not personally made that decision. "Have you asked Christ into your heart yet? Would you like to?" His pleading expression changed to one of relief as he enthusiastically nodded yes. We prayed together right then and there.

I was blessed to be in the congregation when he presented his "new and improved" message. It was meaningful. It was powerful. It was about his personal commitment to Jesus Christ that had been made just days before.

I heard the gospel message that day and I heard the message to never let an assumption of faith keep you from sharing your faith. Simply because this young man was faithful in his church attendance and a kind and considerate individual, I had assumed incorrectly he had a personal relationship with Jesus. Put your faith into the Give Away box. You never know who might take it out.

DRAWING FAITH AS WELL AS WATER

John 4 tells the story of a woman who had a noontime encounter with Jesus at a well. She'd gone to draw water from the well, but she had waited until later in the day hoping the central meeting place for the townspeople would be more deserted.

She was startled to see Jesus at the well and even more surprised when Jesus, a Jew, addressed her, a Samaritan woman. It was culturally known that Jews did not associate with Samaritans. When Jesus asked her for a drink of water and then told her He could supply living water that would quench her thirst forever she was puzzled "Sir, " the woman said, "you have nothing to draw with and the well is deep. Where can you get this living water?" Are you greater than our father Jacob, who gave us the well and drank from it himself, as did also his sons and his livestock?"

Jesus answered, "Everyone who drinks this water will be thirsty again, but whoever drinks the water I give them will never thirst. Indeed, the water I give them will become in them a spring of water welling up to eternal life." She then asked Jesus for a taste of this water and Jesus instructed her to fetch her husband. Confused, she said, "I have no husband." Jesus amazed her by saying, "You are right when you say you have no husband. The fact is, you have had five husbands, and the man you now have is not your husband." In awe, she admitted, "I can see that you are a prophet."

The woman at the well had gone from puzzled to amazed. This stranger knew all about her. When she realized this she put down her water jar and ran back to town to tell the others. "Come, see a man who told me everything I ever did. Could this be the Messiah?"

And the people came. She put her faith into the Give Away box. She shared it with others in town. "Many of the Samaritans from that town believed in him because of the woman's testimony, 'He told me everything I ever did.' So when the Samaritans came to him, they urged him to stay with them, and he stayed two days. And because of his words many more became believers. They said to the woman, 'We no longer believe just because of what you said; now we have heard for ourselves, and we know that this man really is the Savior of the world'" (John 4:39-42).

The Samaritan woman put her faith into the Give Away box and her neighbors took it out. First they believed just because of what the woman said. Then they believed because they knew for themselves that Jesus was Lord. Now they had faith of their own to give away.

REFLECTION
♥
TIME TO CLEAR THE HEART CLUTTER

Did you come to faith as a result of someone putting his or her faith into the Give Away box and extending to you? Take some time to write about that experience. Next, see if you can condense your testimony to an "elevator speech"—your testimony of faith in 60 seconds. Make it concise, brief, and to the point. Make sure it is accurate and compelling because you never know when you will be asked to share about the hope within you.

If you don't yet have faith you can give away, there is no time like the present.

Know that:

○ God is holy and perfect. We are sinners and cannot save ourselves. (1 Peter 1:16; Revelation 4:11; Romans 3:23; Isaiah 59:2)

○ God provided Jesus Christ as the perfect substitute to die in your place. (Romans 5:8; John 14:6)

○ Your response is to receive Jesus Christ by faith as your Savior and Lord (John 1:12-13; 5:24)

You can do this by simply praying:

"Lord Jesus, I need you. I realize I'm a sinner and I can't save myself. I need your mercy. I believe you died on the cross for my sins and rose from the dead. I repent of my sins and put my faith in you as Savior and Lord. Take control of my life and help me follow you in obedience. In Jesus' name, Amen.⁹"

○ Respond to Jesus by living a life of obedience. (Luke 9:23)

♥

11
CHOOSE TO GIVE AWAY PRAYER

The Give Away box was filling up nicely. As I continued to purge the clutter, I found one more thing I could add to the box. I wanted to give away prayer. God's word has a great deal to say about prayer. There are some aspects I understand and some that baffle me. The whole idea that the creator of the universe is ready, willing, and able to talk with me is mind-boggling. More than being available, he actually wants to communicate!

Our kids all went to college about fifty miles from home. I didn't miss their dirty laundry (probably because they did a good job of accumulating it for trips home) and I didn't miss the empty gas tank in the van, but I definitely missed them. More than anything I missed talking with them. While they were growing up, we spent a great deal of time talking to one another. Often, in their high school years, they had kept both John and me up later than usual to discuss something important to them. When they went to college I tried very hard to still be available and distraction-free when they called, but to refrain from calling simply because I was lonely.

It was fun to talk with our kids. It is even better to talk with God. I want to be available and not distracted when I sense God's voice, and in contrast to my sons, He is never annoyed when I call. He is glad to hear from me anytime. He is never too busy, distracted, or disinterested. He is always available, caring, and compassionate. And He wants to communicate with you.

THE HABIT OF PRAYER

Praying for and with your family is a wonderful thing to give away. Almost every morning during the school year as our kids were growing up we ate breakfast together and finished the meal with prayer. For nearly fourteen years John and I fasted each week on Wednesday. On that fasting day we would pray for each other and each one of our sons. Many times there were other concerns we also lifted to the Lord. Although Wednesday was not our only day of prayer that was a day we set aside specifically to give away prayer.

1 Thessalonians instructs the church to "pray without ceasing," but the first time I read that I was puzzled. How could I pray constantly? I was certain bowing my head and closing my eyes would be dangerous if I was driving the car. Yes it would be, but, as I later learned, the verse has nothing to do with the posture of your body. It has everything to do with the posture of your heart. To pray without ceasing is to have a continual God-consciousness regardless of location or circumstances. It would seem God calls us to put prayer into the Give Away box at all times.

My prayers are not fancy. I once heard a woman speak on prayer. She was very articulate and polished and spoke about things like the availability of God and His love. She was so professional that, for just a moment, I started to question whether my regular voice with its regular tone and regular words were sufficient. Praise God the feelings of doubt was short-lived. I soon remembered I didn't have to learn a whole new vocabulary in order to communicate with my Father, my friend. I could talk with Him as simply as a child talks to her daddy.

God relishes your prayers. He wants you to talk with Him. "Let us then approach God's throne of grace with confidence, so that we may receive mercy and find grace to help us in our time of need" (Hebrews 4:16).

BROKEN IN

Years ago John and I bought our first new automobile, a mini van. It only had five miles on the odometer when we picked it up, and it smelled exactly like a new car should smell. When we brought it home I created a rule for the kids, one they had never heard before: No eating in the van until it's broken in.

One week later I filled the van with gas and headed to a weekend conference with two of my friends. The three days we were gone were three days filled with laughing and learning. As we headed for home down a two-lane road in Indiana we all agreed it had been a great trip.

Suddenly a car failed to stop at the crossroad and darted out right in front of the van. When I saw what was happening I immediately slammed on my brakes. We skidded and swerved and rocks flew as the back tires locked and slid onto the shoulder. It was obvious a collision was imminent and we began to pray aloud. "Jesus, help us. Protect us!"

"Protect the driver of the other car."

"Be with us Lord!"

Seconds later there was a loud crash as my van and the other car collided. Both vehicles came to an abrupt halt and all three of us continued to pray for the woman in the other car. Fortunately the van had just grazed her back left bumper and it looked like the driver was unhurt. Our prayers for her safety and ours had been answered.

We had almost avoided the collision. The key word is *almost*. There was minimal damage to the car but the van was another story. Our brand new minivan looked like a very large car-eating animal (a car-nivore, no doubt) had taken a huge bite out of its front. One headlight was hanging by a wire. The grillwork had disintegrated, and mysterious parts were revealed, parts I'd never seen before.

The police were on the scene within a matter of minutes. When I got to the station I called home. "John, I've had an accident. We're all OK, thanks to God."

"How's the van? Can you drive it home?"

At this point I could hear all three of our young sons clamoring in the background. "Is mom OK?" "Can she make it home?"

As John reassured them that I was unhurt and would make it home in a few hours, there was no longer a tone of anxiousness in their voices. In fact, the focus shifted completely and I heard them ask their dad two more questions. "If the van has had a wreck, is it broken in? Can we eat in it now?"

Yes, it was definitely broken in. Bring on the French fries and gummy bears. More importantly keep the prayers coming. Sharing prayer with my friends for the vehicles and lives of all those involved saved us from what could have been a tragic end. Prayer makes a difference. Make prayer your first response and never hesitate to give it away.

ASKING FOR PRAYER

On more than one occasion I have asked someone to give away prayer for me. Long before I became a Christian, I believed in the power of prayer for the really big things. When I was in grade school our kitchen caught fire. I ran next door to Jane's home as her dad ran to ours to begin the fire-fighting process. I was crying and I pled with Jane and her older sister to pray with me so our house didn't burn down. It didn't, and I probably failed to thank Him or even talk to Him again until the next "fire" threatened to consume my life.

Sarah was a foster mom with a great big heart and lots of love. She was the kind of foster mom every kid deserves. Through the years she provided a home for many, many children. Some of those kids were more difficult to love than others though each had their own set of demanding needs. One child in particular came into their home with an even more challenging background. This little boy needed extra prayer. Sarah prayed. Her church prayed. The women's Bible study group prayed. I prayed.

The responsibility of caring for this hurting child was taking its toll and Sarah was becoming especially exhausted. One morning, she stopped me in the grocery store. I could tell she was near the end of her rope as she greeted me with a request. "Do you remember in the Old Testament [Exodus 17:8-16] when Moses held up his arms and the Lord's army prevailed? Then his arms became tired and he let them fall down and the Lord's army began to lose the battle. Do you know that passage?"

Before I could reply she continued. "Aaron and Hur came to Moses' aid. They came alongside of him and helped him hold up his arms to insure victory for the Israelites. Well, I'm no Moses but I can't hold up my arms one minute longer. Will you help me?"

Of course the answer was yes. I pledged to pray daily for the Lord to be at work in the life of this child and to give Sarah strength. In the family of God we can ask for prayer. It is a privilege to give away prayer for one another.

OUT OF ORDER?

Prayer changes things. I know that's true because God's Word declares it. I also know I don't always pray in His will. Occasionally I take over and start giving God instructions. Sad to admit, but it's true.

Years ago I worked long and hard on writing project and finally completed the task. When it was finished I approached several publishers with my proposal. During this time I had asked certain individuals to pray for the acceptance and success of my project. Not long after making that request something dawned on me – something very convicting and embarrassing. *I* had decided to give this project a try and now I wanted God to bless my efforts. *I* had determined my direction without prayer or seeking His will. *Now* I was bringing the Lord into the picture and wanted Him to give me success.

Psalm 37:4 says to "delight in the Lord, and he will give you the desires of your heart." He gives you the "desires of your heart" because a committed life only desires what He wants to bestow. Through God's goodness and grace the project did not succeed. I learned a lesson and God spared me from something He knew was not best. I learned a valuable lesson about praying for God's will before trying to do anything according to my own wishes.

"Pretty! Shiny! Give me!!" Those are the demanding words of the toddler as he reaches for the carving knife on the counter. His parent does not give it to him because the child could be harmed. God, our perfect parent with infinite wisdom, always knows what is best for you.

Ultimate Communication

Prayer is talking and listening. It is communication with your Heavenly Father. Betty, the preschool Sunday school teacher, knelt at the altar to pray after taking communion. The little boy in her Sunday school class was intrigued by this and asked his mother about it in a loud stage whisper. "What's Miss Betty doing?"

"She's talking to Jesus."

"What's Jesus saying to her?"

"I don't know. She probably can't hear Him because of all the noise you're making."

You and I both know that no amount of noise can keep us from hearing the still small voice of God if that's our desire. In prayer we talk and we listen.

I'm no expert on prayer but I am a "pray-er". One of the most important things I have learned through the years is that I pray to *know* the mind of Christ not to *change* the mind of Christ. The more I understand what God desires for me and for those on my prayer list, the more effective my prayers will be.

Unselfish Prayers

Pam is a prayer warrior. The chapter "Choose to Pray" in my book *Live Free* tells about her unselfish choice to pray. As I did research for that chapter I asked if she would share her prayer journal with me. She did and I discovered her prayer list included more than prayers for Emily, her very sick infant daughter. It looked something like this:

- Emily – healing from her tumor

- Russ and Jeanette – overcome marriage struggles

- Keith – successful knee surgery

- Jill – help finding a job after relocating

Day after day her entries looked very similar, prayers for Emily and for others. I was amazed and also a little ashamed as I wondered if my prayer journal would be such a reflection of generosity. She placed prayer after prayer into the Give Away box. How often I have focused only on my own needs or the needs of my family.

Another friend of mine shared prayers for a very difficult person in her life. She had prayed for many years that this individual would come to know Christ as her Savior, but to no avail. Then one day my friend had a thought bigger than one she could have possibly had on her own. "As I prayed for her salvation that day," she told me, "God showed me my motives were wrong. I wanted this woman to become a Christian to make *my* life easier. I didn't really care about her eternal life. I only cared about the comfort of my temporal life."

What a Holy Spirit insight! From that point on, my friend's heart was changed and so was the motivation for her prayers. She discovered that as she gave away unselfish prayers for this woman, she began to feel compassion and love where there had only been indifference. Prayer can change the pray-er!

Sometimes, I know the specific needs of an individual and some-times I just know there is a need. After receiving a call from one of our college-age kids, I learned he was going through a rough time at school. When we hung up the phone I told John I wasn't sure how to specifically pray and we chose to simply lift him and his concerns to God. We prayed that he would somehow be encouraged. The next evening, he called, again, and I decided to inquire very gently about how his day had gone. "It went pretty well. Actually, I saw some guys I hadn't seen all semester and we're getting together tomorrow. It was encouraging." He used exactly the words that had been on our lips as we prayed. The Lord had encouraged him through his friends!

How Can I Pray for You?

Like so many mothers, my children have always been recipients of the prayers I put into the Give Away box. I prayed for them before they were born. I prayed for them in their cribs at night. I prayed for them as they got older and added their voices to mine.

When each son reached the age where he was praying on his own, I knew it would still be important for me to pray. In junior and senior high, many of their concerns went unshared. That was when I began to ask God to help each one make the "Next Right Choice." I didn't need to know what that choice was, I merely wanted them to make the next right choice followed by the next right choice and then the next right choice. When they became adults, I prayed for them from afar.

One year as I broke open my new prayer journal I had an idea. Our sons were all adults now with families of their own. Rather than imagining I knew the concerns in their lives I wrote a quick email to all three sons and their wives and asked how I could pray for them. That question brought amazing feedback. Each of the six kids shared their requests and I not only knew the prayers requests, but I got a beautiful glimpse into each person's heart. What a blessing for a mom and mom-in-law!

Are You Listening?

There once was a young pastor with a teachable spirit and a great deal to learn. One day an older woman from his congregation made an appointment to see him. As it turned out, her reason for scheduling the meeting was to straighten him out in a few areas. After almost thirty minutes of correction and criticism (taken graciously by the pastor) he informed his visitor that he would need to close their meeting in order to take another appointment he had on his calendar. "Would you like me to pray before I leave for my next meeting?"

"I think I'd rather do the praying if that's all right with you." "Certainly. That would be fine."

The pastor bowed his head as the woman began to pray. "Dear God, help Pastor do a better job of visiting like I told him. And give him better sermon illustrations for his shorter sermons. And God, make him a little snappier dresser – and his wife too – and remind him to turn down the thermostat before he leaves on Sunday. Amen."

The self-satisfied congregant raised her bowed her head and looked directly at her pastor. "Well, preacher, did you hear what I just said?"

"Oh, I'm so sorry. I wasn't listening. I thought you were talking to God."

Undoubtedly that permanently ended his counseling sessions with her.

Effectual and Fervent

The prayer of a righteous person is powerful and effective" (James 5:16).

Occasionally the groups I speak to have an intercessor assigned to pray before, during, and after my messages. It's awesome to know people are giving away prayer for me even though we haven't been officially introduced.

I flew to Florida to speak at a one-day, countywide teachers' institute. It was a wonderful experience with a receptive audience of teachers and their aides. I was fortunate enough to meet a woman in particular who was great encourager. During a lunch break, she came up to visit with me and share a story or two that supported the information I had given to the group.

A few weeks after the event, I heard from her once again. Even though the conference was sponsored by a public school district, she had concluded I was a Christian and hence her sister in Christ. Our connection led her to add my name and ministry to her church's prayer list. Every Monday morning for the remainder of the school year a special group of prayer warriors lifted me up in prayer. What a wonderful gift from this Christian friend – this sister in Christ.

My husband prays for me every day. This is a precious gift of love. Jesus prays for me, too! Hebrews 7:25, "Therefore he is able to save completely those who come to God through him, because he always lives to intercede for them."

So does God's Holy Spirit. "In the same way, the Spirit helps us in our weakness. We do not know what we ought to pray for, but the Spirit himself intercedes for us through wordless groans. And he who searches our hearts knows the mind of the Spirit, because the Spirit intercedes for God's people in accordance with the will of God"[10] (Romans 8:26-27).

When we pray we are simply conversing our heavenly Father. It is both talking and listening. No amount of noise can keep us from hearing the still small voice of God if that's our desire.

REFLECTION

TIME TO CLEAR THE HEART CLUTTER

Do you give away prayer for your family and friends? Write down one concern for each member of your immediate family and pray for that concern every day for a month. Note concerns for your extended family and friends (a list that will undoubtedly be much longer) and choose a specific day each week to pray for those concerns.

As you learn God has answered your prayers, make note of that too. Keeping a record of prayer requests and answers is very encouraging.

Knowing someone is praying for you is comforting. Call, text or email one of the people you have been lifting in prayer and let them know you are praying.

Sometime in the next two weeks, ask several people you care about how you can pray for them. List their concerns here and then be faithful to pray!

♥

12
THE GIVE AWAY RULE

The Give Away box now contained more things than I could have ever imagined. When I first began to clear the clutter I didn't know what I might find inside my heart, mind, and memory to give away.

TREASURES, NOT TRASH

Before we move on to the next box, there is a rule you need to know. A little German lady, alias Mom, told me to make sure I only put things into the Give Away box that were useful to others. In other words, her instructions were to give away jewels and not junk; good things, not garbage; and treasures, not trash. In my life I have hung on to many things that were once-upon-a-time treasures but are no longer. Things like the Crockpot that no longer works or the shoes that are well-worn and beyond repair. Maybe you have a collection like this. These are not jewels, good things, or treasures. It's time to get rid of things like these but they *don't* belong in the Give Away box. Don't put that yellowed roll of wrapping paper or your broken toaster into the Give Away box either. And the avocado throw pillows with filling that has long since gone bad will probably do very little to enhance someone else's home.

When I was dejunking my room as a young girl and I discovered a 500-piece puzzle with several pieces missing, I would remember

126

Mom's rule. Give away good things, not garbage. Her rule kept me from putting trash into the Give Away box. Instead it went into the Throw Away box. I can still hear her voice. "Why give away things someone else will just have to throw away? Give away things people will appreciate while they can be appreciated."

When the time came to give away our sons' baby clothes, I found it difficult. In fact I was almost silly about it. We had three healthy boys and I was in my late thirties. The chances were slim we would have another child. It was difficult for my husband to understand my melancholy. "Why don't you just get rid of the baby clothes?"

"I hate to. What if we have another baby?"

"If we do I'll buy him new clothes."

It really wasn't much of a gamble on his part and he was willing to take it in order to regain several square feet of attic space.

Although I've been told that having a garage sale is fun, I've never been convinced. Rather than price the precious little boy hand-me-downs, I sorted through the bags to retrieve special items like the blanket my aunt had made. I also gathered the things that belonged in the Throw Away box. There was no reason to give away shirts that would never come clean or trousers worn thin at the knees and there was no reason to keep perfectly good items that someone could use right now.

As I sorted and sifted through the bags I cried. The little socks and undershirts, pants, and onesies reminded me of an earlier time, a time that had passed and would never come again. They reminded me of change – something that is neither bad nor good but is inevitable. Our boys were growing and changing almost every day and it was time to share those pieces of clothing with someone else. It was time to put the good things into the Give Away box.

To console myself as I worked on the task before me, I imagined the scene of a mother-to-be opening the boxes and examining her "new" treasures. "Oh! Look at this little shirt. It's so tiny! And this beautiful blue outfit – my son will look so handsome in this. And these blankets are so soft and just like new! These things are exactly what I need!"

Experience Needed

Mom's rule also applies to the things that go from your heart, mind, and memory into the Give Away box. When you clear the clutter it's important to put things into the correct box. You may have had an experience that could have no positive worth to another human being yet you are tempted to share it. Maybe giving away that experience will illustrate how smart, talented, or extraordinary you are – or think you are. It could be that your desire is to elevate yourself. Ugh! That might seem a little harsh but it is food for thought.

You may have known a person who tends to share too much information, much more than has been requested. I can fall into that category. When I hear an answering machine ask for my name, number, and a brief message, it's easy for me to ignore the word "brief." I am more inclined to leave something akin to an epic novel than a few quick sentences letting the recipient know I called and why. It is likely that the long message contains information of no particular use or even of interest to the listener. By sharing these unsolicited comments, I run the risk of puffing myself up and giving away trash. I am learning to honor the request for a "brief message" after the tone.

128

Likewise, if your experience is of no use to the listener, it is best to avoid putting it into the Give Away box. Remember to give away experience and wisdom as they are requested. Also remember to avoid giving away an experience that could hurt another person.

MEMORY LANE

The memories we create have the potential to be either good things or garbage. You cannot always make a perfect memory for your family or friends, but if a positive memory is your goal at least you're aiming at the right target. My husband has been known to say I never have a disaster, "just another story to tell." That's pretty accurate, although I did come very close to witnessing a disaster on a family vacation years ago. The memory of the event still causes me to shudder.

Our family decided to take a vacation to Alaska. Early one morning, we boarded a bus with several other Denali National Park visitors and took an eight-hour trip into the tundra wilderness to see the wildlife. We were fascinated with the adventure as we spotted sheep, elk, and the highlight of the day—a huge grizzly bear. We stopped and the tundra native lumbered down a creek bank crossing the road between the two buses. How exciting it was to witness this massive animal and snap several photos before he disappeared from sight. Little did I realize that the excitement of this encounter would soon pale in comparison with what was to come.

After the bus tour ended, we drove to a large rock formation to do some climbing. Then we headed down a gradual slope to the riverbed. It was a braided river which meant rather than one stream, there were multiple, shallow tributaries and tiny branches which were twisted together. The boys began skipping rocks and walking upstream. The two older boys could easily jump over the narrow alleys of water and the youngest one jumped as far as he could and kept as dry as possible. John and I climbed back up the slope and rested at a picnic table about three hundred yards from the river.

As we sat there visiting with one another and enjoying the gorgeous scenery, a car drove up and a man frantically jumped out. "There are two male grizzly bears running down the riverbed!" At first, his warning did not register with either of us. He repeated the information with increased intensity. "There are two male grizzlies in the riverbed coming this way!!" When he didn't get a satisfactory response from us he shouted with full-blown urgency, "Are those your kids down there? The bears are running right toward them!!!" Finally the message hit home.

John left my side and raced toward our kids, yelling to get their attention. The wind muffled his shouts and the boys, looking down at the river, couldn't hear him. He continued to run and yell. As he did, I could see the first grizzly coming although he was still many yards away.

Our youngest son saw his dad first. He didn't know what John was saying, but he knew something was wrong, so he started to run toward him. Our middle child looked up watching his little brother run by. Then *he* saw John and heard only one word—*BEAR*! That, combined with the panicked look on his dad's face, was enough of a clue. He took off toward safety like a gazelle. Our eldest son was the farthest upstream and still hadn't heard his father's cry. Oblivious to his brothers' desertion, he looked up in the direction of the racing bears. By now, both of male grizzlies were visible. One glance at the galloping beasts sent him off in rapid pursuit of safety. Within seconds, he'd caught up to one of his brothers. As he ran beside him, he pointed out that books recommend you stand completely still if

130

a bear approaches. His brother's reply? "Fine. Go ahead. Then they'll eat you first."

By this time the first bear was about fifty feet from the boys. Amazingly, the massive animal made a ninety-degree turn and took off up the mountainside. The second bear followed. It seems his mission had been to chase bear number one from his territory. Neither of the grizzly bears was interested in the boys or what they were doing.

Only seconds later everyone reached my side. At that point I was extremely emotional. As we stood together, the bears continued the chase up the slope and were eventually out of sight. I was praising God for the protection and trying to regain my composure when the boys became a little emotional too. Their emotion, however, was not fear or relief. It was sheer exhilaration.

"Wow, that was great!"

"Did you see how close that first bear got to us?"

"Man, I didn't know you could run that fast!"

They had survived a near-attack and were loving it! A disaster? Absolutely not! The five minutes when I was experiencing sheer terror was one of the highlights of the trip for them and a memory none of us will ever forget. The challenge for me was to see the episode as a positive memory. With a sense of adventure and a sense of humor, many memories can become good ones to give away.

JEWELS OR JUNK?

Authentic encouragement is a jewel. Perhaps the only time it might warrant a trip to the Throw Away box instead of the Give Away box is when the encouragement is insincere. If you assure someone that her red hair is truly lovely and she has black hair, your encouraging words will definitely be suspect. Encouragement must be genuine and have no ulterior motive in order to belong in the Give Away box.

Faith in Jesus Christ and prayer are good things to give away when the emphasis is correctly place. If the emphasis is on you, the giver, then you might want to rethink the gift. It just might be junk. If your desire is to elevate yourself or illustrate your superior spiritual nature, even faith and prayer can fail to be jewels or treasures. Pay attention, as you sort through the clutter in your heart. The Give Away box should be as full as possible but don't let vanity and selfish ambition sneak into it. As you clear the clutter, remember the rule for the Give Away box.

To some who were confident of their own righteousness and looked down on everyone else, Jesus told this parable: "Two men went up to the temple to pray, one a Pharisee and the other a tax collector. The Pharisee stood by himself and prayed: 'God, I thank you that I am not like other people—robbers, evildoers, adulterers—or even like this tax collector. I fast twice a week and give a tenth of all I get.'"

"But the tax collector stood at a distance. He would not even look up to heaven, but beat his breast and said, 'God, have mercy on me, a sinner.'

"I tell you that this man, rather than the other, went home justified before God. For all those who exalt themselves will be humbled, and those who humble themselves will be exalted."[11]

If your desire is to elevate yourself or illustrate your superior spiritual nature, even faith and prayer can fail to be jewels, good things, or treasures. You have to pay attention as you sort through the clutter in your heart. The Give Away box should be as full as possible but don't let any throw away items sneak into it. As you clear the clutter, remember the rule for the Give Away box.

REFLECTION

TIME TO CLEAR THE HEART CLUTTER

When you give away experience, God can use it for good. But here's a tough question – Have you ever given away your experience to manipulate someone? Here's another tough one – have you ever given away an experience to elevate yourself? Write down the answers to those questions. If the answer to either or both of them questions was yes, admit it and ask God for forgiveness. Record just enough of the facts to be a reminder to only give away treasures in the future.

It is important to give away jewels, not junk. No one needs more trash, more negative clutter. Has anyone given you something that should have been put into the Throw Away box instead? Write down that experience. What did the trash look like/sound like? Now that you've identified the garbage it's time to throw it away yourself. And remember, no digging in the trash.

♥

13
LET'S KEEP THESE THINGS

My Keep Box was the smallest of the three. I had found several things for the Give Away Box and the Throw Away Box was filled to overflowing. Now it was time to determine which things I should keep. As I sorted through the remaining clutter, I realized there was one very important thing I had inside of me that I wanted to keep. That one thing was the word of God. It couldn't even be classified as clutter. In fact, the Word had played a big role in helping me determine the fate of the things I had previously discovered in my heart, mind, and memory.

HIDE IT IN YOUR HEART

In Psalm 119:11 we are told that hiding God's Word in our hearts (putting it into the Keep Box) will help us avoid sin. Sin is a definite source of clutter. Putting God's Word in the Keep Box can help you avoid accumulating that clutter.

The young woman knew she was making a poor choice. She was so sure her actions were wrong that she made a conscious decision to avoid evaluating their appropriateness. What was she doing? She was flirting with a young man at work. Actually, she was flirting with adultery since, for *she* was a married woman. "I'm not doing anything wrong," she argued with herself when her conscience was pricked. "He's just a friend, that's all. There's nothing wrong with having a friend."

And so the "friendship" grew. They took time to visit each day at their 10 o'clock coffee break, and eventually started eating lunch together. Once in awhile, the woman would feel a touch of guilt, but she was able to stifle those feelings and convince herself the meetings were completely innocent.

One day she felt particularly upset about the growing relationship and decided it would be best to seek counsel. She thought it might be a good idea to have a little help sorting out her feelings. Unfortunately she did not know the admonition of Psalm 1, or she simply decided to ignore it.

"Blessed is the one who does not walk in step with the wicked or stand in the way that sinners take or sit in the company of mockers, but whose delight is in the law of the Lord, and who meditates on his law day and night" (Psalm 1:1-2).

Though commanded not to "walk in step with the wicked" or as the New King James Version says, "walk not in the counsel of the ungodly," the woman sought the counsel of someone whose lifestyle mimicked her own poor decisions. Instead of objective and moral counsel, her behavior was encouraged to continue in the inappropriate relationship. Ultimately, the woman got the advice she wanted, but rather than wise counsel, it was agreeing counsel. That guidance ultimately ended her employment with the corporation and almost ended her marriage. Hiding God's Word in her heart could have given this bad beginning an entirely different ending.

Hiding God's Word in your heart can help keep you from sin.

"Direct my footsteps according to your word; let no sin rule over me" (Psalm 119:131).

YOUR WEAPON OF CHOICE

"Take the helmet of salvation and the sword of the Spirit, which is the word of God" (Ephesians 6:17). God's Word is your sword, your weapon in battle with the enemy. With God's word, you can silence Satan and uncover his tricks.

The devil had the gall to try tempting Jesus himself! You know what He fought him with? The Word. Matthew 4 says, "Then Jesus was led by the Spirit into the wilderness to be tempted by the devil. After fasting forty days and forty nights, he was hungry. The tempter came to him and said, "If you are the Son of God, tell these stones to become bread. Jesus answered, quoting Deuteronomy 8:3. "It is written: 'Man shall not live on bread alone, but on every word that comes from the mouth of God" (Matthew 4:1-4).

Jesus let Satan know that his time of fasting and consecration would not be cut short by any tricks, no matter how much his human nature fought against him. Dissatisfied, Satan tried again. Identifying Jesus' strategy of using the Word to win, he tried it, too, by quoting Psalm 91 out of context.

Then the devil took him to the holy city and had him stand on the highest point of the temple. "If you are the Son of God," he said, "throw yourself down. For it is written: "'He will command his angels concerning you, and they will lift you up in their hands, so that you will not strike your foot against a stone.'"

Jesus fired back Deuteronomy 6:16: "It is also written: 'Do not put the Lord your God to the test.'"

This time, Satan had attempted to manipulate Jesus into jumping off of a cliff to prove his proclaimed power. But, yet again, the Word silenced him. Tenacious by nature, Satan tried one last time to tempt Jesus.

Again, the devil took him to a very high mountain and showed him all the kingdoms of the world and their splendor. "All this I will give you," he said, "if you will bow down and worship me. Jesus would have nothing to do with the tempter and responded with 1 Chronicles 21:1, "Away from me, Satan! For it is written: 'Worship the Lord your God, and serve him only.'"

The Word of God, the sword of the spirit, won the battle. "Then the devil left him, and angels came and attended him" (Matthew 4:11). By the power of the Word, Jesus was victorious over Satan. He gave us that same Word so that we can be victorious over the enemy, too.

Sadly, I have witnessed times when the Word was used as a lethal weapon directed toward another person rather than toward evil. I've heard scripture quoted not to remind the speaker or the listener of the truth, but to impress, depress, and or repress. But, that isn't how God intended the weapon of His Word to be used. It's to be used to triumph over evil and the evil one.

Encouragement Extraordinaire

I can still remember the look on the faces of about a dozen adults when we were challenged to memorize Psalm 139. "Memorize?"

"The whole thing?"

"You're kidding!"

138

"I can't!"

"You're kidding, right?"

"I won't"

"I'm too old!"

"We're not going to have a quiz on this, are we?"

"Please tell me you're kidding!"

There was no kidding and they were assured there would be no quiz. The assignment was simply to commit this chapter of the Old Testament to memory; to practice hiding God's word in their hearts. Why? Because the Word is encouraging and can be powerful when it is applied to life itself.

The Perfect Instructor

The Word of God is a "lamp to my feet and a light for my path."[12] It illuminates my path, keeps me from sin, equips me for spiritual battle, encourages me, and it also gives me instruction. Paul wrote, "Finally, brothers and sisters, whatever is true, whatever is noble, whatever is right, whatever is pure, whatever is lovely, whatever is admirable—if anything is excellent or praiseworthy—think about such things."[13] Conversely, whatever is untrue, dishonorable, inappropriate, impure, hideous, or contemptible – if anything is inferior or disreputable – do NOT think about such things. The Bible says that as a man "thinks in his heart, so is he."[14] Your thoughts are very important. The items placed into the Keep Box have a great influence over you. Soon enough, what you think turns into action and behavior. God's Word can correct your sinful thoughts before they become sinful actions.

PICTURE THIS

God's Word also helps you have a more accurate picture of Him. Maybe you've heard stories of how little children have described God. Those are often entertaining. "I don't know too much about God, but I do know His first name. It's Howard. You know, 'Our Father who art in Heaven, Howard be thy name.'"

Several years ago there was a popular cartoon series entitled "Dear God." It was based on fictitious letters from kids to God. The ideas were cute and served to remind the audience of the fresh uncultured way kids address the Lord. The cartoons did not necessarily give an accurate picture of God, but the true picture can be derived from scripture.

In the very first chapter of the Bible, we see that God is the creator.[15] He created all things[16], including you, in His image. (See Genesis 1:27.) He can create love where there is no love and, as creator, he can repair what seems irreparable. He can create life and bless a husband and wife with a child.

Exodus 34:14 shows us that God is a jealous God and commands there to be no other gods before Him.[17] That includes your husband, your kids, your profession, money, power, and prestige. All of those things can become gods, placing them in a higher priority than the Lord. Remember, you cannot serve two masters.[18]

God is merciful.[19] He is gracious and compassionate[20]; He is forgiving[21];He is righteous[22]; and He is faithful[23]. He is spirit[24]. What a wonderful picture! God is all those things and more. He blesses you, disciplines you, and is your refuge. (See Deuteronomy 15:6; 8:5; 33:27.)

140

I remember when a young man in our youth ministry got a better picture of the true nature of God. We had taken the teenagers to a two-day conference in a city about two hours from our community. It was a great way for everyone to bond and to grow spiritually. As the kids piled into my van for the trip home, I welcomed them with my typical greeting. "I want everyone to think of one thing you learned over the last two days. I want you to share at least one thing that caused you to think." The teenagers were used to these "reflective sessions" and usually humored me by participating. Each of the passengers took some time to think about my challenge and then shared an insight.

One teen girl told me about a key idea from a purity workshop she had attended. Another talked about what she had experienced as the worship songs were sung. One of the last to share was a young man who'd received a life-changing epiphany.

"You know what hit me? It was something the main speaker said about some verse in Psalms. Wait, I wrote it down. Let me look it up. 'How precious to me [or concerning me] are your thoughts, O God! How vast is the sum of them! Were I to count them, they would outnumber the grains of sand. When I awake, I am still with you.' What an awesome thing! God's thoughts concerning me are so numerous that they outnumber the grains of sand! That's a whole lot of thoughts. He cares for me *that* much!"

From Psalm 139, this teenager had caught a glimpse of an accurate picture of God and His love. He realized God was so filled with love and concern for him that He thought of him countless times. That is a picture of God, compliments of His Word.

The picture you have of God could be influenced by the picture you have of your earthly father. No biological dad can adequately resemble

141

your perfect Heavenly Father. Unfortunately, some biological fathers have very few attributes resembling God. Be on guard and don't be confused. Make sure your picture of God is based on information from the Bible.

"COMFORT YE MY PEOPLE"

Another plus of placing God's Word in the Keep Box is the comfort it delivers.

I visited a young woman in the hospital. As I entered, I quietly greeted her parents who were keeping vigil at her bedside. My friend was very ill; too sick to even know I had arrived. Her body was filled with tumors that were visible through her thin hospital gown.

The gown, though it weighed almost nothing, caused her discomfort as it touched her thighs and torso. With her hands at her side, she slowly and deliberately gathered up her gown to relieve the pressure it created. Underneath she was naked, and as the gown inched up to her midsection, her mom gently pulled it down to provide a degree of modesty.

In her pain, modesty did not matter. As soon as her gown was pulled down and smoothed over her body, she began to hike it up again. I sensed her mother needed my assurance. "It's OK. I want her to be as comfortable as she can be."

That was all Mom needed to hear. She left the gathered gown around her daughter's midsection. As I left the hospital room that day, knowing I had seen my friend alive for the last time, I remembered a portion of scripture that spoke directly to me.

"Who shall separate us from the love of Christ? Shall trouble or hardship or persecution or famine or nakedness or danger or sword? As it is written: "For your sake we face death all day long; we are considered as sheep to be slaughtered."

No, in all these things we are more than conquerors through him who loved us. For I am convinced that neither death nor life, neither angels nor demons, neither the present nor the future, nor any powers, neither height nor depth, nor anything else in all creation, will be able to separate us from the love of God that is in Christ Jesus our Lord" (Romans 8:35-39).

This young woman who loved Jesus would never be separated from Him. As she lay dying, she could be comforted by that truth. And as I grieved, it was also a comfort to me.

PROMISES, PROMISES

The verses that comforted me also gave me a promise, one that will never disappoint. By putting the Word into the Keep box, I am storing the promises of God in my heart. All of those promises are in the scriptures. His promises are different from the ones I make. Although I try my best to keep my word, I sometimes fail. I don't always remember a promise I've made and sometimes I'm unable to honor a promise because of circumstances I didn't anticipate.

God always keeps His word. It is flawless[25] and will stand forever[26]. God's promises are guaranteed. One of God's most powerful promises is that of eternal life. John, a disciple of Jesus, wrote, " For God so loved the world that he gave his one and only Son, that whoever believes in him shall not perish but have eternal life."[27] If you believe in God's one and only Son, Jesus, you will have the greatest gift God ever gave.

The Lord also promised He would give you peace. He told you in His Word what to do and what not to do. "Do not be anxious about anything, but in every situation, by prayer and petition, with thanksgiving, present your requests to God. And the peace of God, which transcends all understanding, will guard your hearts and your minds in Christ Jesus."[28] You can exchange worry for thankful prayer.

God's promises never change because He never changes. "Jesus Christ is the same yesterday and today and forever" (Hebrews 13:8). Putting God's Word into the Keep box means you have the weapon you need to combat sin. You have an overwhelming source of encouragement. You have an accurate picture of God, His comfort, and the knowledge of His promises.

Ponder the following passages:

"Praise the Lord. Blessed are those who fear the Lord, who find great delight in his commands" (Psalm 112:1).

"I will never forget your precepts, for by them you have preserved my life" (Psalm 119:93).

"The grass withers and the flowers fall, but the word of our God endures forever" (Isaiah 40:8).

Reflection

Time to Clear the Heart Clutter

Do you have some of God's Word hidden in your heart? Recall several of your favorite verses and write them here.

Commit to hiding even more of the Word in your heart. How about Psalm 139? You can do it!! Write it down in this space and let the learning begin.

What have you been thinking about today? Take time to write out Philippians 4:8. Now think of one example for each description.

In your own words, describe God.

♥

14
THE KEEP PARADOX

As I gently placed God's Word into the Keep box, I had an *Aha!* moment. I realized that many of the things I had put into the Give Away box I could keep too. It was a paradox.

RESPOND OR REACT

A response is a thinking reply. A reaction is more like a knee jerk — no thinking involved. I've learned from experience that it's wiser to respond than react in most situations. My experience has been gained from both good and bad choices. Read on for an example of one of those bad choices, a time when I chose to react.

One summer, our family took a vacation to New York City. Because we live on a farm in central Illinois, this adventure was very different from our daily lives. During the few days we spent in the city we did all the typical tourist things including a trip to the top of the Empire State Building. After that particular excursion, we walked across the street to dine at - *sigh* - a fast food restaurant. I've heard there are some unforgettable dining spots in the Big Apple, but on that special evening, our choice was to eat in someplace that was affordable and familiar.

As we approached, the woman behind the counter looked at me and gave me the traditional head nod indicating it was my turn to order. "We'd like a number eight with an oran-"

Before I could finish the sentence, a man who had merged into our line spoke up. It was the security guard from the Empire State Building. This uniformed and armed diner gruffly interrupted me in mid-sentence. "I'm next!" The interruption startled me and not only did I stop speaking, I quickly began to back away. The woman behind the counter was not startled and spoke calmly to the agitated guard. "No, you're not. This lady is next. Go ahead, Lady." Her words were accompanied by the head nod.

I began again, a little more tentatively this time. "We'd like a number eight, with…"

"Hey, Lady! I said I was next!!" Trust me, I was willing to let him go next, but the unruffled cashier had a different idea. She shook her head no and turned back to me, indicating I should place my order once again. At this point I was questioning exactly how many number eights we'd be receiving. "We'd like a number…" My meek attempt to order once again was all it took to send the highly impatient security guard into a shouting fit. He yelled obscenities I had never heard before or even imagined. He called the woman behind the counter ugly, disrespectful names and shouted crude things with increasing volume.

In my shock, my reactions took over. With no thinking whatsoever, I quickly leaned forward across the counter and gently patted the arm of the dear woman who had been trying to take our order. Then in a very loud voice I expressed my feeling about the guard's outburst. "No one deserves to be spoken to in that manner!"

It was very clear how I felt about the man's colorful vocabulary. But I had forgotten two significant things: (1) This was New York City

148

and not the small rural village I call home; and (2) The very rude guard was packing heat. He was armed and possibly even dangerous! As I was leaning and patting the cashier and indirectly chastising the ill-mannered security guard, my family was tugging at me, trying to get me to stop. Can you see the headline I might have been creating? "Midwestern Woman Gunned Down by Security Guard." It would have been assumed he felt I was a security risk when, in actuality, I was just a sympathetic woman who'd reacted, emotionally, to his foul mouth and rude behavior, rather than responding logically.

Thank goodness that headline never made the paper. The guard turned around in a huff and left the restaurant. I was safe, in spite of my actions. As I reflected on the incident, I realized how foolish I had been. It reinforced my commitment to respond rather than react, regardless of the situation. This was an experience I put in both the Give Away and Keep boxes.

RECYCLED MEMORIES

Memories can be placed in both boxes too. You may recall the Fat Fairy. The two of you were introduced several chapters ago. The Fat Fairy performed many acts of kindness and generosity in our home. I let you in on the poorly kept secret that I am the official Fat Fairy. I am the official one, but not the first one.

I grew up in a home that was frequented by the Fat Fairy. She left money for teeth I had lost; she hid the Easter Eggs; and she presented each member of our family with a gift at Christmas. My mother was the Fat Fairy in our home. She created a wonderful memory for me so I put it into the Give Away box for our kids and grandkids to enjoy. I gave away the memory and I've kept it.

Encouragement to Give Away and Keep

As I headed north and west on the Tri-State toll road going around Chicago, the traffic was bumper to bumper. I never experience traffic like that where I live except for a few minutes of congestion after the Sweet Corn Festival parade. If you live near a much larger metropolis you are used to the congestion and the ritual of stop-and-go traffic as each driver pays the toll and heads down the road.

I didn't have exact change or an I-Pass, so I edged my way over to the manual lane. As I slowly approached the tollbooth, I could see the woman who would soon take my dollar and give me change. When it was finally my turn I handed her a dollar bill, and the most amazing thing happened. The tool booth lady spoke to me. Trust me, this is highly unusual. Typically there is no conversation except for an occasional grunt in reply to my "Thank you."

"Did you see that car in front of you?" This was obviously a rhetorical question. The car in front of me was only inches away and had been almost that close for several miles. As I pondered the meaning of her question, she continued. "Well, he was talking on his *cell-u-lar* phone and he wanted a receipt. He didn't even have the *guh-ray-cious-ness* to ask for one. He just snapped his fingers at me!"

At this point I was awestruck by the fact that I was actually having a conversation with a tollbooth lady. This was history in the making—an event that would in all likeliness, never be repeated. Simultaneously, I realized I had a brief moment to formulate and deliver my reply. I had mere seconds to encourage this woman who had been discouraged by the driver in front of me. My mind racing, it finally came to

150

me. I looked up at her, extended my hand to receive the change, and shook my head with disgust. "My, my! What would his mama say?"

She thought for just an instant, then smiled and laughed at the thought of the rude driver's mother scolding him for his behavior. It worked! She was encouraged. I was able to dish out the encouragement I'd been storing in the Give Away box and she took gladly accepted. In the end, we were both encouraged. She realized that not all of mankind was rude and self-serving, and I was encouraged knowing I had encouraged her.

KEEP THE FAITH (AND GIVE IT AWAY)

My brother-in-law lay in a hospital bed, dying from a cancerous brain tumor. Every other day, I visited him and read to him. His hospital room was filled with Scripture verses I had printed and every time I went to see him we prayed together. During one of those times the chief oncology nurse asked to see me in an adjacent room. Before she'd spoken a word her countenance let me know she had serious business to discuss. "You must stop praying for your brother-in-law to be healed. He is extremely ill and it is time you faced reality!"

The lecture shocked me for just a minute, but I rapidly came to my senses. "Do you know who Shadrach, Meshach, and Abednego are?" My question drew a disgusted headshake. "They are three men who lived in Old Testament Bible times. These three men made the very unpopular decision not to bow down to an idol made by Nebuchadnezzar, the King of Babylon and ruler of the nation. This choice made Nebuchadnezzar unhappy, furious actually, and he ordered the men be thrown into a furnace if they wouldn't cooperate and worship him.

"The three men were not intimidated by Nebuchadnezzar's threats and told him so. These men declared, 'If we are thrown into the

151

blazing furnace, the God we serve is able to deliver us from it, and he will deliver us from Your Majesty's hand. But even if he does not, we want you to know, Your Majesty, that we will not serve your gods or worship the image of gold you have set up.'[29]" They continued to worship God and were eventually thrown into the furnace. Beyond all odds, God protected them and they came out of the fiery furnace unharmed." After I'd finished my impromptu Bible lesson I guided the nurse to my main point. "The God I know and worship is very capable of healing my brother-in-law. He can do anything He chooses to do. So I am asking Him to do that miracle. And even if He doesn't, I won't stop loving and serving Him. Face reality? He IS reality."

The nurse sat across from me and stared in disbelief. The reality in my life was and is the reality of Jesus Christ. I chose to celebrate life until there was no more life for my brother-in-law on this earth. When that occurred there would be plenty of time to grieve.

Only days before that encounter with the nurse I had shared my faith with my brother-in-law. I had put my faith into the Give Away box and he had snatched it out. From that point forward, the reality in his life was also Jesus Christ. It's a paradox. I gave away my faith and kept it too. I had it to share with the nurse that day.

Unceasing Prayer

Many times when you put prayer into the Give Away box you will speak to God on behalf of someone else. You give away intercessory prayer. You keep the knowledge of the power of prayer and the ability to speak with God, whenever and wherever, in prayer, in praise and adoration, in confession, and in thanksgiving. The wonderful thing about prayer is that it is never exhausted or "used up." There is no finite number of words or petitions allowed.

Let me tell you a story of the college student who volunteered to help a friend. This friend needed someone to babysit her 7-year-old daughter for several hours on a Saturday afternoon. After two hours of serving as the resident adult, this college student was exhausted. The young child had talked nonstop since her mother left for the afternoon and the incessant conversation had made the sitter weary. Finally, after three hours of continual chit chat, the desperate student came to the end of her rope. "Christina, did you know that you only get a limited number of words to use each day? I thought you might like to keep that in mind because you're using up your words really fast."

The young girl thought about this revelation (deception, actually) and decided she had better be quiet and save some words for later, when her mom got home. Needless to say, when Mom arrived and learned of her daughter's newfound (incorrect) information, she was not too happy. There is no limit to the number of words you can speak.

Likewise, there is no limit to the frequency or number of words you have available to talk with God. You can put prayer into the Give Away box, with plenty left for the Keep box. Effectual, fervent prayer makes a difference. I once heard someone say, "When I get to heaven and find out just how much my effectual, fervent prayers *did* avail, I will wish I had prayed more!" Remember, there is no limit!

REFLECTION

TIME TO CLEAR THE HEART CLUTTER

What have you learned from your experiences that you can give away AND keep? Maybe it is an experience that contributed to your wisdom. Write down those experiences, both good and bad.

Share a memory you want to give away to your children, grandchildren, nieces or nephews. The good news is that you can keep it too!

Journal about a time when you gave encouragement to someone and it encouraged you, too. You gave it away and kept it!

Has your faith been bolstered as you gave it away to someone who gladly embraced it? Note a time when that happened. If you are unable to think of one, open your heart to the possibility of it happening soon.

♥

15
ONE MORE RULE

The task of clearing the clutter from my heart, mind, and memory was almost complete. The process was going well and things were looking better than before I began. Just as I was about to declare the job complete, I remembered one more rule Mom taught me. This rule isn't fancy and it isn't unusual. In fact the chances are great that just as my mom taught this rule to me, your mom taught it to you, too, and you may have taught it to your children. I did.

KEEP IT CLEAN

The rule is: When you get it clean, keep it clean. The logic is obvious, but the task is quite challenging. It's a great idea but I have often found it difficult. If you have ever sorted through the clutter of the "junk drawer" by your refrigerator only to find that in six months, or even six weeks, the contents of the drawer are a mess again, you know the challenge. If keeping a drawer in the kitchen free of clutter is difficult, how can you manage to keep your heart, mind, and memory clean?

One Sunday I received an insight into the answer to that question. It was during a small group time. The leader asked us to open our Bibles to Luke 19:1-8 as he read the passage for the lesson.

Jesus entered Jericho and was passing through. A man was there by the name of Zacchaeus; he was a chief tax collector and was wealthy.

He wanted to see who Jesus was, but because he was short he could not see over the crowd. So he ran ahead and climbed a sycamore-fig tree to see him, since Jesus was coming that way.

When Jesus reached the spot, he looked up and said to him, "Zacchaeus, come down immediately. I must stay at your house today." So he came down at once and welcomed him gladly.

All the people saw this and began to mutter, "He has gone to be the guest of a sinner." But Zacchaeus stood up and said to the Lord, "Look, Lord! Here and now I give half of my possessions to the poor, and if I have cheated anybody out of anything, I will pay back four times the amount."

What did this lunchtime meeting with Jesus have to do with Mom's rule – When you get it clean, keep it clean? It would seem Zacchaeus had never even thought about the things he was accumulating in his heart, but he had heard that Jesus was coming to town. Since he was a short he knew he would need to find a good spot if he hoped to see what was happening. He climbed up a tree and, sure enough, he saw Jesus. Not only that, but Jesus saw him!

This didn't please everyone in the crowd. Several of the onlookers were hostile and let Jesus know in no uncertain terms that by choosing to eat with Zacchaeus he was on his way to be the guest of a sinner. [Quick sidebar: Unless Jesus ate alone, he was always the guest of sinners as none is perfect and sin-free but Him! I guess they didn't realize they were sinners, too. See Romans 3:23.]

I can imagine their disdain.

"I have a roast in the oven, Jesus. Wouldn't you like to come over to *my* house for dinner?"

"I'm a very good cook, Jesus. When we have potluck at church I never bring home any leftovers."

"I can't believe Jesus would want to eat with Zacchaeus. He's a no-good, dirty tax collector!"

"And I just got new carpeting. I had to pay a premium to get it installed. Now Jesus isn't even coming over. He's going to be the guest of that awful man."

He realized the possibility existed that the things the townspeople were muttering were not very flattering. After all, he had lived a life with no regard for pleasing God with his actions or decisions. Now He was provided the opportunity to spend time with the One who could help him change his life. If their criticisms were accurate, he needed to examine his life and make some changes. By the same token, some comments may have simply been malicious gossip. A few of the mutterers might have been giving him trash instead of treasures, trash that belonged in the Throw Away box.

Some of the muttering Zacchaeus heard was useful, helpful stimulus for change. Some of it was trash. Which words were valid? Which words were garbage destined for the Throw Away box? It is important to differentiate between the two because…

(1) What if you throw this clutter away and then discover you need it to shape your life, making you more like Christ?

(2) What if you keep it and it is only junk?

158

Even though it seemed as though Zacchaeus had never cared about the cleanliness of his heart, he gives an illustration of what you can do to answer those two questions correctly. Read how Zacchaeus responded to the mutterers. "But Zacchaeus stood up and said to the Lord, 'Look, Lord! Here and now I give half of my possessions to the poor, and if I have cheated anybody out of anything, I will pay back four times the amount.' He spoke to the Lord and not to the people. He took it straight to the top and asked the Lord to help him know the truth and act on it—and if I have cheated anybody out of anything, I will pay back four times the amount.'"

When you hear the muttering of others take it straight to the top. God knows if it is truth to act upon. There is no need to address those who mutter. Zacchaeus was off to a good start. He was preparing to clean up his heart and he set a good example for each of us.

The key to keeping it clean is to identify the truth. Jesus, the one who is the truth, will help you do just that. Finding the truth in each instance will help you put the input where it belongs. Any helpful words can become agents of change. Any that are untruth can be discarded before they enter your heart, mind or memory. There's no need to take in garbage, trash, or junk.

CLUTTER CONTROL

When I clear off my desk each day I have the option of opening the top drawer and simply sliding all the clutter directly into it. Then if I am able to actually shut the drawer and I shut it quickly I might be able to convince myself I've sufficiently handled the junk. Sure, it will be out of sight and my desk will mess-free, but the reality is that there is still a mess I'll have to face later. If I take the time to determine the appropriate spot for each item on my cluttered desk, and put those things where they belong, I'm more likely to keep it clean.

Zacchaeus' encounter with Jesus showed him how to evaluate the muttering/the clutter. He now wanted a clean heart so he asked the Lord what changes should be made and what comments were just junk. What a great example for those of us who want to maintain a clean heart. Even though that is my intention, I'm not always diligent to keep my heart clear of clutter. Sometimes I try to dialog with those who are muttering and persuade them that their criticism is misdirected. That usually gets me nowhere.

It's far better to take it straight to the top. The Lord knows what you need to take into your heart. He knows what changes you need to make and by the same token, He will protect you from the things that belong in the Throw Away box. It is as simple as saying, "Look, Lord, if I have done this thing, if I have acted selfishly, if I have been arrogant or self-centered, if I have done anything from vain ambition or selfish conceit, then please tell me. I want to be a woman of God. I want to be more like you."

God loves you! In fact, He's crazy about you and He only wants the best for you. If you start to question that, dig out His Word from the Keep box and be encouraged. You know His true nature. When He prunes and nudges you, when He disciplines you, it is done lovingly and gently and for your own good. God loves you!

By the same token, if He lets you know that some or all of the muttering is not relevant or applicable, you don't have to let the clutter into your life. Instead it belongs in the Throw Away box. If you allow it to enter your heart you'll only have to sort through it and throw it out later.

Take it straight to the top. Let the Lord guide you, like he did Zacchaeus. God will help you get it clean and keep it clean.

REFLECTION

TIME TO CLEAR THE HEART CLUTTER

Jot down the circumstances in which you found yourself the subject of muttering. What was your reaction or response? Get clarity and peace by taking your concern straight to Jesus. Seek the mind of Christ on this issue and record the actions you will take.

CONCLUSION

❤

In the future, my hope is to gather many more treasures to give away. My experiences increase with each passing day, as does my wisdom, gained from both good and poor choices. Through them, I want to generously give away encouragement, memories, faith, and prayers. I know I am never limited to how much I can give. Betty, a missionary whom my husband's family has known for years, always greets us with the same question: "What has Jesus been doing in your life lately?" After we answer, we repeat the question to Betty. It's a comfort to know that, as life continues, I will have new accounts, jewels of God's work in my life, to share. And I will be blessed by the accounts of other believers.

Remember your prayers can never be depleted. When you find yourself dealing with false guilt, anger, arrogance, shame, and other emotions that belong in the Throw Away box, God is there to instruct you, comfort you through His Word, and re-direct you. Train your mind to have a God-consciousness at all times, "praying without ceasing", so that the enemy doesn't have victory over you with His lies and temptations.

When you get it clean, keep it clean and no digging through the trash!

YOUR CHOICE

Choosing to clear the clutter from your heart, mind, and memory is not easy, but it is not impossible. It's your choice whether you give away good things not garbage. It's your choice to refrain from digging in the trash. It's your choice to keep it clean.

No person can force you and God will not force you either. He will, however, equip you for the task and encourage you in the process. That is precisely what He's been doing through the centuries.

May your heart, mind, and memory be cleared of the clutter that will hold you back. May you be filled to overflowing with the goodness of God.

ABOUT KENDRA SMILEY

 Kendra Smiley is a popular speaker and author, passionate about helping others "Make the Next Right Choice." The always-active former Illinois Mother of the Year hosts a daily radio show, *Live Life Intentionally*, heard on over 350 stations. A sought after national and international speaker, she addresses thousands of women each year. Kendra and her husband John, a retired USAFR pilot, live on a farm in central Illinois. They have three married sons and ten grandchildren.

(Endnotes)

1   Isaiah 55: 8, 9.

2   1 Corinthians 13:5

3   *Phillippians 2:3*

4   *Genesis 4:8*

5   1 Thessalonians 5:11

6   Ephesians 4:29

7   Acts 4:36-37

8   2 Corinthians 6:14

9   *More Than Winning: Discovering God's Plan for Your Life –* Fellowship of Christian Athletes, 1986)

10   Romans 8:26-27

11   Luke 18:9-14

12   Psalm 119:105

13   Philippians 4:8

14   Proverbs 23:7

15   Genesis 1:1

16   Colossians 1:16

17   Exodus 20:3

18   Matthew 6:24

19   Deuteronomy 4:31

20   2 Chronicles 30:9

21   Nehemiah 9:17

22   Romans 1:17

23   1 Corinthians 10:13

24   John 4:16

25   Proverbs 30:5

26   Isaiah 40:8

27   John 3:16

28   Philippians 4:6-7

29   Daniel 3:17-18

Made in the USA
Lexington, KY
11 August 2017